1. 45

LOGOTHERAPY

LOGOTHERAPY

An Evaluation of Frankl's Existential Approach to Psychotherapy

by
Donald F. Tweedie, Jr.

BAKER BOOK HOUSE
Grand Rapids, Michigan

Library of Congress Catalog Card Number: 61-17221

Copyright, 1961, by
BAKER BOOK HOUSE

ISBN: 0-8010-8780-5

First printing, September 1961
Second printing, October 1965
Third printing, February 1972

PHOTOLITHOPRINTED BY CUSHING - MALLOY, INC.
ANN ARBOR, MICHIGAN, UNITED STATES OF AMERICA
1972

TO
NORMA

FOREWORD

The occasion of this pleasant task of examining Logotherapy was provided by the granting of a sabbatical leave from Gordon College. It is directed at no particular group of readers, but rather is a report of a personal inquiry. Thus, any lack of systematic analysis, or comprehension of critical evaluation, may be attributed to the fact that it is presented just as it developed in the author's experience.

An especially great indebtedness to Professor Frankl is hereby acknowledged. His friendship and encouragement, as well as the gracious commitment of his time and the facilities of his clinic, have been a prime factor in the work of this volume. Personal thanks are also extended to his staff at the Vienna Polyclinic for the countless ways in which their assistance and courtesies have contributed to the completion of this task.

DONALD F. TWEEDIE

Logotherapy is not a closed, but rather an open, system and theory. It is prepared for the evolution of itself as well as for the cooperation and coexistence with other schools of psychotherapy. There are no ready-made solutions of age old problems which Logotherapy has to offer; this teaching rather represents a challenge to psychiatry, and perhaps also to theology.

For the benefit of its evolution, Logotherapy needs a team of experts to stimulate and guide its development. I regard Dr. Tweedie, an authority in his field of religious psychology and counseling, to be one of those experts. Inasmuch as I am no expert in this area I do not regard myself competent to judge his professional skill, but what I do consider myself capable of evaluating is the authenticity of his endeavor. This is what impressed me most deeply during the period of our working together in Vienna.

Therefore, the saying of a Chinese sage holds true for me with respect to him: "The blame of a wise man is to be esteemed higher than the praise of the many." I would say, listening to those who acclaim us is blinding; listening to those who criticize us is enlightening. That is why I do not mind, but on the contrary value, the criticism of the author. Throughout my life I have learned through my disciples and pupils at least as much as I have taught them. The Latin dictum of ancient time, *docendo discimus,* is still valid; it should merely be enlarged by including both teaching and treating, i.e., theory as well as practice concerning people in despair. Then we can watch and witness that by administering consolation we are consoled, by comforting we are comforted, or to put it again in Latin: *consolendo consolemur.*

I personally doubt whether, within religion, truth can ever be distinguished from untruth by evidence which is universally acceptable to man. It seems to me that the various religious denominations are something like different languages. It is not possible, either, to declare that any of them is superior to the others. Similarly, no language can justifiably be called "true" or "false," but through each of them truth — the one truth — may be approached as if from different sides, and through each language it is also possible to err, and even to lie.

The more weakly one stands on the ground of his belief the more he clings with both hands to the dogma which separates it from other beliefs; on the other hand, the more firmly one stands on the ground of his faith, the more he has both hands free to reach out to those of his fellow men who cannot share his belief. The first attitude entails fanaticism; the second, tolerance. Tolerance does not mean that one accepts the belief of the other; but it does mean that one respects him as a human being, with the right and freedom of choosing his own way of believing and living.

Viktor E. Frankl, M.D., Ph.D.

TABLE OF CONTENTS

LOGOTHERAPY AND THE CHRISTIAN FAITH

CHAPTER I

INTRODUCTION

One of the great tasks of modern man lies in the field of mental health. He is called upon, in a time of unprecedentedly rapid social and technological change, to safeguard the emotional stability of himself and his fellow men. In addition, there is the responsibility of attempting to rescue those who have lost their moorings and are foundering in the sea of mental and emotional upheaval.

That this is no small task may be seen at a glance. More than half of all our hospital beds are in the service of the mentally ill, and these are astonishingly short of the demand. One person out of every eleven in our population will spend some time in an institution for the emotionally disturbed. Even without a proportional increase in the incidence of illness, the burgeoning population would, like the mechanical rabbit at the dog tracks, keep the goal of meeting the needs of the ill inevitably out of reach. There is evidence to indicate that there has been no increase in incidence in the last few years, but this gives little comfort, not only in view of the population increase, but also in the fact that so many people are forsaking the fear of social stigma and are presenting themselves for treatment.

Of course, not every person who experiences emotional instability needs to be confined to a hospital ward. The out-patient clinics and private offices of therapists must often assign the applicants for treatment to long waiting lists, or infrequent visits, in order to avoid a flat refusal. The number of those who are defeated in the meeting of problems along life's way is so great that Flanders-Dunbar estimates that 80% of our population would profit by psychotherapeutic treatment! That this number will not soon lessen may be assumed by the increase of family mobility and instability, the immensity of the problem of juvenile delinquency, and the pressure of racial and economic tensions. These factors as well as, on the international level, the wars and rumors of wars will assure the aspiring young psychotherapist of the necessary clientele for a long and busy practice.

On the other hand, the corps of professionals in the field of mental health is woefully small. These are also poorly deployed, being concentrated around a few large urban areas of population. Many, if not most, of these are oriented to psychoanalytic methods of treatment and thus the picture is complicated by their practically interminable analyses, and the resultant paucity of patients whom they are able to serve. In addition, the high cost of private therapy tends to exclude from the field of fiction the remark that "only the rich can afford neuroses."

On the positive side of the ledger, however, there seems to be some basis for encouragement. The needs of the mental health program are not hidden under a bushel, but rather are being shouted from the housetops. Local mental health associations are springing up all around us. Laymen have rushed in where clinicians feared to tread and have enlisted the aid of women's clubs, church groups, veterans' organizations, and various and sundry societies to join the forces to stamp out mental illness. These mental health associations are soliciting funds, broadcasting information, establishing clinics, and setting a climate of opinion that hopefully will eventuate in an emotionally prophylactic atmosphere in homes and schools, and adequate treatment for those in need.

Training facilities for professionals are also being expanded and psychologically trained personnel are, in spite of the absence of the blessing of the medical profession, gradually assuming more responsibility in the field. The advent of the psychotherapeutically oriented minister and institutional chaplain is a recent phenomenon which is already paying dividends in the alleviation of emotional distress among parishioners and patients. Vocational counselors and school psychologists are providing guidance in the educational systems, and will, hopefully, redeem innumerable potential personal failures among their charges.

Workers in the field of research have also not been standing idly by. Those convinced that "behind every twisted thought lies a twisted molecule" are engaged in an all out effort to locate the physical factors of stress and strain, and their alleviation. "Tranquilizing" and "energizing" medications have to a degree replaced the techniques of "shock" and psycho-surgery. Blood factors have been isolated which may reveal the inner secrets of psychotic adjustment. On the psychological level, new theories, or new developments of old ones, are published with such frequency that one is hard put to keep abreast of them. A recent volume presents 36 different techniques of psychotherapy and apparently many of these will be later subdivided.[1] A fairly recent development is that of group therapy, which, while it has not always demonstrated its validity, at least promises to make treatment available to more people.

In view of the pressing need to alleviate the emotional ills of man in the modern world, and the activity already underway to this end, it may appear to be fiddling while Rome burns to attempt to re-evaluate the presuppositions of psychotherapy, and to add any new approaches to the already confusingly long list of psychotherapeutic "schools and scholars." However, activity does not necessarily indicate progress, and it is unquestionably true that backtracking may be the only means of making real headway if one has started in the wrong direction.

In spite of the increasing number of personnel and the intense research in the area of causal factors, diagnostic theories, and treatment techniques of mental and emotional disorders, there has been too little progress made. The best established methods of dealing with emotional ills seem little better than chance. A study[2] revealed, for instance, that, among the patients who were on the waiting list of a psychotherapeutic clinic, there was as high a proportion of improved cases as among the patients treated! Inasmuch as treatment is so expensive, and the time and expense of training therapists so extensive, it may seem that it would be on the part of wisdom merely to let the patients alone. Surely the improved persons of the treated and untreated groups of the above mentioned study represent the same category of "those who will get well" — it would seem a terrible indictment of the therapeutic profession if the opposite

---

[1] Harper, Robert A., *Psychoanalysis and Psychotherapy — 36 Systems*, Prentice Hall, 1959.

[2] Saslow, G., and Peters, A., *Psychiatric Quarterly*, vol. 30, 1956.

were true, and the "failures" of the therapists were those
who would have recovered if left alone!

Rather than to bow in easy resignation, however, it would
seem appropriate to examine the "material" of the psychotherapeutic craft. It is undoubtedly true that the view of
man which the therapist holds, whether implicit or explicit,
will influence his approach to the problems of man. "Every
psychotherapy is based upon anthropological premises, or, if
they are not conscious, upon anthropological implications."[3]
Diagnoses and treatment methods must of necessity be related to the essential structure of the subject of the application — man himself. Often the question, What is man? is
shrugged off as being too naive to require response, or else
is received with the uneasy suspicion that something "metaphysical" will be involved in the answer. It is much easier to
get busy helping man and leave the problems of the philosophy of man to those who spend their working hours in
armchairs.

A. *Philosophies of Man*

In spite of the innumerable variations in anthropological
presuppositions, it is possible to designate a few central
theories that tend to summarize man's thinking about man.
Some of them sound rather recent in the history of thought,
but upon investigation turn out to be ancient theories, having appeared in the earliest literary efforts, and now and

---

[3] Frankl, HB, 665. Each reference to the works of Prof. Frankl
will be noted with such a key and page number. The explanation of
the key, as well as full bibliographical data, will appear at the end of
this volume under Bibliography. All quotations from German writings are translated by the author with an effort made to safeguard
the contextual significance.

then reappearing, garbed in contemporary verbiage more befitting the scientific era. The ancient Greek thinkers brought them first to light, and they have since waxed and waned in popularity, but never have expired.

1. The Mechanical Man

The first is what may be called the physicalistic view of man. A human being is regarded as a chance concatenation of physical particles in a universe containing only "atoms and the void." This view was first presented by Leucippus and Democritus, before the time of Socrates, and has held a place of prominence throughout the course of recorded history. Man is a machine whose functions are to be understood as the movement of bits of matter in space and time. Every aim and aspiration, every joy and every sorrow, is but an instance of action and reaction, attraction and repulsion, exemplary data of physical laws. The new, intricate, and fascinating electronic computers are not really different from the engineers who make them: they are just more crude, less sensitive in certain respects, and much more accurate. Every thought and every desire of man is merely the occasion of material complexes, logically no more nor less significant than the friction of two grains of sand in the Sahara Desert.

This view of man has been made popular and pervasive in the twentieth century in the area of academic psychology by Watson, and the behaviorists who have followed in his train, denying the existence of consciousness and the many personal human experiences, in their more extreme assertions, or else assigning them to a vague "epiphenomenal" status, which apparently has no "parts or passions." The important contributions of Pavlov and other reflexologists have made the study of man a safe and secure "natural science" which need not blush with embarrassment in the presence of its older brethren, physics and chemistry.

This satisfaction is short lived, however, when one considers the consequences. Those human treasures of ethics, ideals, and love, are exchanged for the fools' gold of a reductionism which changes them to mere moments in a field of material forces. This is not to say that man does not have an extremely important physical dimension, but rather that this dimension does not exhaust his nature and his potentialities. Neither does this assertion exclude the value and usefulness of the research of the behavioristic psychologists. It demands, however, that behaviorism shall not overlook that significant level of behavior which is evidenced when one tells a naughty child to behave himself. Conversely, only a fool would say the same thing to a watch which was not keeping good time.

In the field of mental health, the value of decisiveness and human aspirations ought to be too well realized to be beguiled into the inexorable and pitiable fatalism that is entailed in the theory that man is only a physical machine. It is a tragic joke that may be readily observed in the literature affirming such a view of man, which presents the physicalistic view as a *fact*, as something that *should* be believed, and marshals arguments in order to *convince* the reader. However, in the theory itself there is room neither for truth, obligation, nor decision. "At first man understood himself as a creature, and, to be sure, after the image of his creator, God. Then the machine age came, and he soon began to understand himself as a creator, and, strange to say, after the image of his creation, the machine!"[4]

---

[4] Frankl, MS, 46.

The physical factors in human personality are very important. A small change in the secretion of a gland, or the function of a group of nerves, can greatly change the behavior of an individual. The field of chemotherapy will, no doubt, continue to be of inestimable value in psychotherapy. However, these factors should not be permitted to loom so large that they overshadow and obscure those essential characteristics of human personality which make man "a little lower than the angels" and give him a citizenship in a realm qualitatively far removed from sticks and stones and shifting sand.

2. THE PHYLOGENETIC MODEL

Another widely held view of man regards him as a complex biological organism. His physical characteristics are appreciated, but not permitted to obscure the fact that he has a feature which is not found in the complexes of matter, and is unexplained by the rules and principles of physical theory — he is alive. Though the gulf between the organic and inorganic has seemingly been narrowed by biochemical research, yet is it still wide and deep when one observes the difference between the living and the dead. While the inanimate slowly drifts in disintegration to an entropic wasteland, the living struggles to stem this tide by utilizing bits of this material world into means for survival and reproduction. This point of view was not unknown to the pre-Socratics, but it was Darwin, a century ago, who gave it form and impetus for our time. There is a great living evolutionary realm which had a modest and secret beginning in some prehistoric swamp and which, sometimes by slow, imperceptible, accidental variations, and sometimes by mysterious and sudden travail, through which offspring as "out of due time" appear, has eventuated in the vast interrelated complex kingdom of flora and fauna, with self-conscious and rational man upon its throne.

There is much to commend this description of man. The success of the Gestalt psychologists in biological and psychological research, and the "organismic" work of Goldstein and others, have made the "bundle hypothesis" of the physicalistic theory of man a bit difficult to retain. The "purpose" revealed in the metabolic process, and the "ingenuity" of the healing process in man, certainly demand a higher principle of explanation than mechanism. Thus in the biological view, the "dust of the earth" is transformed into marvelous organic entities, the highest of which, man, has created intricate social institutions and complex technological tools in his struggle to attain his goal in life. This goal, when viewed from that anthropological perspective which holds that man is essentially a biological specimen, is survival, accompanied by its necessary counterpart, reproduction.

Once again, however, man is presented in a truncated fashion. His highest achievements, and noblest aspirations, are reduced to the mundane plane of cellular activity. His social accomplishments are merely accidents of the instinctive drive toward his biological end. His rational moments, which burst the bonds of space and time, are designated as spatio-temporal instruments of the biological thrust. Even when he contradicts the basic thesis of survival by committing suicide, it is considered as one of those exceptions that somehow prove the rule.

3. The Rational Animal

Of those who thought the foregoing exceptions were too hard a test for the rule, the most familiar is Socrates of ancient Athens. Convinced that man was more than a complex of "flesh and sinew," he, followed by his student and literary spokesman, Plato, led the way to a view of man in which the highest and noblest dimension reflected and appreciated the good, the true, and the beautiful. The biological structure which provides the plaguing drives and passions is a "prison house" of the true aspect of man — the rational and immortal soul. Man is essentially man only when he is thinking. His defects and problems are erased when ignorance is eradicated. His true nature is expressed in the attainment of rational ends.

This "classical" view of man survived the middle ages and bloomed in the Renaissance, but has been hard put in modern times to survive the avalanche of enthusiasm for natural science. Anything that is not available to the traditional five senses has been ignored by the modern anthropologist and psychologist, as they respond to the "status drive" to Natural Science. Anything so resembling superstitious metaphysics might cost them their membership. In educational circles this anthropology has had a slight revival under the enthusiastic leadership of Mortimer Adler and his Great Ideas, but otherwise it has short shrift. In the field of mental health one may occasionally observe unconscious acceptance of a rational view of man in the abortive attempts to "educate the public." It is also sometimes presupposed in the therapeutic hour in the hope that when the patient "knows his own dynamics," then he will be all right.

The almost universal acceptance of a primary unconscious component of man in contemporary psychology seems to obviate the possible resurgence of man as primarily a thinker. However, the increasing interest in Ego Psychology may be also increasingly fruitful if the rational aspects of the unconscious mental process receive due consideration. In any

respect, "life is deeper than logic" and this necessary corrective to the view of man as exclusively physical and/or biological must not usurp the throne of a onesided anthropology.

4. THE IMAGE OF GOD

Another view of man, which has had an even longer
history than the foregoing, is that emphasizing his religious
nature. Before the concepts of the Greeks were crystallized,
a religious anthropology stemming from the Hebrew tradition was firmly established. This held that the truly important aspect of man was that he was a creature of a Divine
Being, and in some way made in His image. Man's highest
function and purpose in life is to worship his Creator and to
serve Him. Various religious concepts from other cultures
tended to blur this particular religious view of man, but it
was this biblical concept, as it was extended through the
development of the Christian church, which by and large
undergirded the cultural development of western civiliza-
tion for the last two millennia.

The last century has witnessed a progressive repudiation
of the spiritual nature of man, however, and an exclusive
emphasis on his physical factors has taken its place. This
emphasis seemed to be more in accord with the precepts of
modern science, and seemed to offer a greater hope for new
insights in the area of mental and emotional strength.

Such has been the secularization of our culture that Allport has noted the strange situation today whereby people
will, with candor and without inhibition, discuss the most
intimate details of sexual experience, but would blush to
confess a religious impulse.

There has been of late, however, a surge of interest in
the religious interpretation of man in the field of psychological

and psychiatric research which, if not to the proportion of "turning the tide," is nonetheless receiving a wide and serious hearing. The sterility of theories and techniques based upon man conceived as a mechanism or psychological apparatus has given an air of necessity to the reviewing of what, until recently, was considered a dead option.

B. *Psychology and Religion*

The relationship between psychology and religion is presently, at least in America, one of the more popular topics of discussion, both by the workers in either of the two fields and by the general public. Seminars on psychology and religion are held in hospitals, churches, theological seminaries, and university classrooms. Theological schools are busily introducing ministerial students to the complexity of the human psyche and to the clinical care of the ill. Psychologists and psychiatrists are becoming increasingly sensitive to theological concepts,[5] while ministers, seeking better means to understand and to assist their parishioners, are becoming more aware of, and more willing to accept the fruits of, psychological research. Organizations, such as the Academy of Religion and Mental Health, and the Christian Association for Psychological Studies, have become, in less than a decade, well co-ordinated movements in this interdisciplinary research.

Such a rapprochement was generally considered, during the first decade of this century, an impossible syncretism, a fellowship of light and darkness. This was due, to a large

---

[5] Cf. "Sin and Psychology," *Time*, Sept. 14, 1959, p. 35. This article points up the surprising interest and significance given to a symposium on "The Role of the Concept of Sin" at the annual convention of the American Psychological Association.

extent, to the overwhelming influence of behaviorism, psychoanalysis, and philosophic positivism, which reduced man to a mechanism of reflex arcs, or instinctive drives, and excluded by way of presupposition any possible transcendence to a realm of spiritual values. This realm was considered the ghost of a superstitious era, and no proper source for scientific data. Religious experiences were evaluated in terms of automatic responses of the organism to its present material environment. On the other hand, theologians, already on the defensive before the aggressive thrust of modern technology, immediately repudiated psychology as the work of the devil, and the results of its research as statistical irrelevancies which would only hinder the work of the church. There was a great gulf fixed between the secular university department and religious organizations over which, apparently, no man could, or would, pass.

The pressing problem of mental health seems to have precipitated the present attempt to bridge this gap. The growing awareness of the inability of either discipline to comprehend the whole man and his needs in times of sickness started the "conversation." The pragmatic benefits of religion as a therapeutic ally, and a prophylactic force, have extended the relationship to the level of courtship. A marriage seems imminent, if not already consummated, as "psychological sermons" go forth from the pulpit, and in at least one major university a faculty member holds appointment in both the theological and medical faculties.

It may be premature to announce the millennium, however, for this frequently threatens to be only a marriage of convenience which ultimately will serve the ends of neither partner. Psychology yet often seems to pay mere lip service to religious experience. A materialistic psychological system can do no other with a system which is based upon spiritual

concepts. The latter must of necessity be secondary rationalizations, or frank delusions, as long as they are held to be
essentially meaningless and nonexistent. On the other hand,
religious thinkers sometimes tend to wrench psychological
research from its scientific mooring in order to provide a
better alignment with their religious preconceptions. One
may occasionally observe the trend to seek for religion the
empirical respectability for which psychology traded its birth-
right of philosophical self-consciousness for the pottage of
positivistic verification.

It appears that there must be a mutual concept of the
nature of man before a true union, or, which may be pref-
erable, a true cooperation, is possible. To this end the existential psychology of Prof. Viktor E. Frankl promises to be
a significant contribution inasmuch as it is based, not upon
a view of man as an exclusively materialistic bundle of drives
and reflexes, but rather, recognizes a truly spiritual dimension
in human personality.

Dr. Frankl is a professor of neurology and psychiatry at the
University of Vienna, and director of the neurological and
psychotherapeutic department of the Vienna Polyclinic. He
is the author of several books, contributor to many scholarly
journals, and an international lecturer. Frankl's consistent
theme has been to challenge those in the field of psychotherapy to treat the emotionally ill as persons, not mechanisms of instinctive drives, and to appeal to inner spiritual
resources of the patients in dealing with them. His efforts
have culminated in what is known as the "third Viennese
school of psychiatry" after Freud's Psychoanalysis and the
Individual Psychology of Alfred Adler.

Frankl's view of man, and his approach in the treatment
of mental illness, is no armchair philosophy, nor textbook
eclecticism, however, but rather, is the fruit of years of

clinical experience. Experience which was obtained through the treatment of thousands of patients in a modern psychiatric clinic, and personally confirmed in the grim nightmare of a Nazi concentration camp.[6] Here was seen on every hand the "borderline situations" (Jaspers, *Grenzsituationen*) of human experience. Here the height and depth of human existence was brought to light in the observation of fellow prisoners who continually existed under the Damoclean swords of disease, starvation, and the gas chamber. Here human nature, with all its high potentiality, as well as its crippling limitations, was revealed in crystal clear perspective. Here was the acid test for a psychotherapy, carried out under threat of punishment, and in the midst of conditions which contraindicated almost every textbook requirement for successful therapy.

Subsequent chapters will discuss Frankl's theoretic and psychotherapeutic concepts, and consider their particular relevance to a Christian *Weltanschauung*. The latter should not be construed as any "official" theological position, but rather, the author's personal conclusion based upon a study of the biblical data. The former concepts are also not "official," although gleaned from Frankl's writings, as well as through many pleasant hours of personal conversation and clinical observation with their author.

---

[6] For a gripping account of some of these experiences, the reader is referred to *From Death-Camp to Existentialism*, Beacon Press, Boston, 1959.

CHAPTER II

LOGOTHERAPY
ITS ROOTS AND RIVALS

A. *Logotherapy and Logos*

Frankl's school is referred to as *Logotherapy*, or *Existential Analysis*. These terms are nearly synonymous and refer to two facets of the same theory. While Existential Analysis is more indicative of the anthropological direction in which this theory is developed, Logotherapy is more descriptive of the actual therapeutic theory and method.

In view of the numerous nuances and variations in the meaning of the Greek word, *logos*, care should be exercised to avoid initial misunderstanding. Though Frankl, as any other therapist, intends that his approach to patients be logical, he in no wise presumes to treat them by means of logic. Logotherapy is not a method of persuasion *per se*, but rather, in many ways is the exact opposite. Neither does Logotherapy refer to the level of reason or understanding, although it is intended to be both reasonable and understandable. Rather, *logos* is taken in the twofold sense of "meaning" and "spirit." On the one hand, it refers to the necessity of meaningfulness in human experience. In this respect, Frankl often uses the descriptive expression, "will to meaning" (in contrast to psychoanalytic "will to pleasure," and Adlerian "will to power"), which is seen as the basic tendency of the unconscious, as well as the conscious spiritual dimension of man. On the other hand, Logotherapy also refers to this spiritual factor itself, which subsequently will be seen to be the cornerstone of the structure of this "third Viennese school." In whatever precise context the term is used, however, it is meant to call attention to the fact that the most significant experiences of man are beyond the level of the merely psychological.

One must be careful at the outset not to consider Logotherapy as a specific religious therapy just because it declares the importance of the spiritual nature of man, and holds to the objective validity of religious values. It is possible that some might misconstrue Logotherapy as essentially Christian inasmuch as the word "logos" is of central significance in the Christian world view. Christ is presented in the New Testament as the incarnate Logos, which, in turn, is identified with God. Therefore, for the Christian, all meaning and value is realized through Christ, the Logos, and authentic existence is found only in Him. Thus it is conceivable that a hasty conclusion might assume the identity of Logotherapy and a specific Christian therapy.

The alternate title, Existential Analysis, is related to the contemporary philosophical movement, existentialism. Herein existence refers to a special mode of being, one which is distinctive of being human. "For this special kind of being, contemporary philosophy has reserved the expression 'existence,' and we have, in Existential Analysis, or Logotherapy, borrowed this term for that content."[1]

To exist is to make decisive judgments and commitments. Only man is able both to choose for himself and, also, to choose himself. This exclusive faculty is the essence of true humanity, and the ground of Existential Analysis.

However, Existential Analysis does not really attempt to analyze this existential aspect of human personality, which neither can be analyzed nor synthesized. This "core" of personality, like the first principle of Aristotle, is not demonstrable. "Existence never stands before me as an object, before my eyes; it stands, rather, behind my thinking, behind me as a subject. Existence is, in the last analysis, a mystery."[2] It is a phenomenological first principle and Existential Analysis is the explication of it.

Existential Analysis analyzes the human personality in terms of his existential possibilities and responsibilities. Basic aspects (*Urphaenomene*) of existence are made explicit: spirituality, freedom, and responsibility. It should not be overlooked, however, that the person, the one "being human," really makes himself explicit, while the analyst observes. He unfolds himself in the course of life. "Just as an unrolled tapestry reveals its unmistakable pattern, we are able to read off the life course, the development, and the essential characteristics of the person."[3]

Existential analysis proceeds from this fact. Frankl does not conceive of his theory as the mere explication of any particular existing person, however, but rather also the explication of existence itself. "In this sense Logotherapy is an attempt to construct a psychotherapeutic anthropology, an

---

[1] Frankl, HB, 663.
[2] Frankl, HP, 11.
[3] Frankl, HB, 664.

anthropology which precedes all psychotherapy, and not only Logotherapy."[4] Thus Frankl declares that Existential Analysis is not just an ontic analysis, that is to say, an analysis of particular patients, or individual ontic entities; but rather, is an ontological analysis of "being human." Therefore, one may presuppose its basic theses whenever he confronts any individual patient.

Logotherapy approaches psychotherapy with the spiritual in man as its starting point; in Existential Analysis the spiritual "core" of personality is brought to the focus of the patient. In short, Logotherapy proceeds from the spiritual, while Existential Analysis proceeds toward the spiritual. It reveals the spiritual nature of man, while Logotherapy meets the objections which are subsequently presented in lieu of facing the resulting responsibility placed upon man by this revelation. These co-ordinate factors blend into a theory which, one may well suppose, may have much in common with a specific religious system such as Christianity. The validity of this supposition will be examined subsequently in reference to anthropology, motivation, and therapeutic goals.

Due to the fact that there is a danger of confusing Frankl's school with other philosophic and/or psychotherapeutic movements, the term, Logotherapy, generally will be used, rather than Existential Analysis. A brief discussion of the historical context of Logotherapy will serve to make this danger clear, and also help to orientate the reader to the seed bed out of which Logotherapy has bloomed.[5]

---

[4] Frankl, HB, 664.

[5] For a fuller, more technical discussion of the relationship of Logotherapy to contemporary European existential philosophy and psychotherapy, see Korger, M., and Polak, P., "Der geistesgeschichtliche Ort der Existenzanalyse": Handbuch der Neurosenlehre und Psychotherapie, Urban & Schwarzenberg: Münich and Berlin, 1959, pp. 632-662.

B. *Logotherapy and Existential Philosophy*

Soren Kierkegaard is usually given the honor, or the blame, for first bringing to the attention of modern man the fact of his existence. Early in the nineteenth century this "melancholy Dane" rose up in protest against the hypocrisy of the two significant social leaders of his day, the pastor and the professor, and against the decadence of his age. He maintained that the pastor neither practiced what he preached, nor encouraged his parishioners to do so. Faith was reduced to being baptized and learning the catechism. Membership in the state church satisfied the social demands of "christendom" and substituted for the crossbearing of Christianity. The vital, personal, suffering "crises of the Christ" were petrified into ecclesiastical creeds.

Meanwhile, "Herr Professor" was holding forth, to his students and to the world, an objective philosophical system. In this system reason was the king, and Hegel was his counselor. Kierkegaard rebelled against this kingdom which had no room for the individual human being. He deplored the folly of Hegel, who "built a beautiful palace, but who must live outside in a hovel." Reality was presumed to be accurately understood only when one was "objective" and had no personal interest in it. Man was depersonalized to a thinking mechanism with neither selfconsciousness nor personal existence.

Against what he considered the great false doctrines of the academic world, "truth is objectivity" and "the real is the rational," Kierkegaard asserted that "truth is inwardness, subjectivity" and "the real is the individual!" "The individual was being swallowed up on the rational side by Hegel's vast logical 'absolute Whole,' on the economic side by the increasing objectivication of the person, and on the

moral and spiritual side by the soft and vapid religion of
his day."[6]

It is not surprising that the reactionary writings of this
rather eccentric, and often emotionally unbalanced, man
should have, in his day, little effect upon the climate of
opinion in Copenhagen. He predicted that he would be
"entirely ignored" and, except for being lampooned by a
local humor magazine, suffered through the truth of his
prediction. But, in seeming demonstration of the biblical
expression, "except a corn of wheat fall into the ground and
die, it abides alone," the works of Kierkegaard have been re-
vived in the twentieth century and have "brought forth
much fruit." His theses have had a remarkable influence in
the areas of theology, philosophy, and psychology. To Kierkegaard more than to any other, but with the assistance of
many others, including Nietzsche, lies the responsibility of
making *Existenz* the *Zeitgeist* of today. "The existential
question in its 'modern' form, thus the 'problem of modern
man,' was raised for the first time by Kierkegaard. What he
had demanded in the nineteenth century, was made possible
and was actualized in the twentieth century."[7]

This existential question, What is man and the meaning
of his existence? in terms of philosophy, was made possible
by the philosophy of "life" of Bergson, and the phenomenology of Husserl and his pupil Scheler. Bergson's *elan vitale*
brought to the attention of philosophers the vital thrust of a
flowing, continuous reality, which is prior to all attempts to
divide it up into neat, static (and to that degree, false),
logical concepts. Phenomenology emphasized the need to
study man's conscious experience without prejudice and

---

[6] May, Rollo, et al, *Existence*, A New Dimension in Psychiatry
and Psychology, Basic Books, Inc., New York, 1958, p. 25.

[7] Frankl, LE, 4-5.

without reservation. Wundt had been right in insisting that introspective analysis is a significant means of understanding man, but he selected only the data that suited the needs of his rigid structural components. The phenomenologists, on the other hand, attempted to take data at face value without a deadly reduction to fit preconceptions.

After the first world war, this new possibility of approaching the existential question was actualized by Heidegger, Jaspers, and Sartre. In the wake of the second world war, it is now even upon the lips of the man on the street. To answer this question, and subsequently, to help the man on the street to discover the answer, is a primary purpose of Logotherapy.

Obviously there is a major difference between inquiring into the meaning of existence in the intellectual atmosphere of the philosophical seminar room and in the existential atmosphere of the psychotherapeutic clinic. However, it is not only the setting which separates Frankl from the various schools of existential philosophy. Whereas modern existential philosophers, perhaps intoxicated by Kierkegaard's "dizziness of freedom," make of the basic freedom of human personality an absolute open choice in the arena of possibility, Frankl insists that existential freedom is not "freedom from," but rather, is "freedom for" something and "freedom before" somebody. "Human freedom is neither identical with omnipotence nor with arbitrariness. And therein Existential Analysis differs essentially from most existential philosophies, but especially from French existentialism."[8] "The talk (of existential philosophy) is always only of freedom, and, if necessary, concerning what man is free from, but never whereto he is free, of his freedom to responsibility."[9] For

---

[8] Frankl, TT, 175.
[9] Frankl, LE, x.

Frankl this responsibility of man is for the fulfillment and actualization of meaning and value. This is the correlative of every decision and all freedom.

Sartre is especially defective with respect to this important aspect of existence, and Frankl specifically denies any dependence upon him.[10] Instead of having to shoulder the meaninglessness of life, as in Sartre's view, one has, rather, only to face up to the indemonstrability of the ultimate meaning. He compares Sartre's attempt to have man "design" himself without a pattern, or to construct a workable nihilistic ethics, to an Indian rope trick, whereby the fakir throws up a rope and tries to make the audience believe that someone then can climb it. From an immanence philosophy, man knows neither what he is, nor what he should be. "Thus he cannot 'design' himself nor 'discover' himself, as an existentialistic atheism supposes. The true discovery of man, the *inventio hominis,* occurs in the *imitatio Dei.*"[11]

Although Frankl is more impressed with the phenomenological analyses of Heidegger and Jaspers, and admits some dependence upon Heidegger,[12] he believes that ultimately they are confined to an unconvincing freedom and decisiveness in man without the necessary objectivity, and, conversely, to a transcendental knowledge and concept of truth without the necessary subjectivity. Frankl would, I think, believe that a paraphrase of Kant's famous maxim would be pertinent in this philosophical situation: "Subjectivity without an object is empty; objectivity without a subject is blind."

In short, the German existentialists are considered to have failed to, convincingly, synthesize their excellent phenomenological analyses with their convictions of transcendental

---

10 Frankl, TT, 170.
11 Frankl, LE, 64.
12 Frankl, TT, 170.

truth and reality. This is, of course, not to deny that Heidegger and Jaspers have made a most important contribution to the history of thought, nor that Logotherapy has received significant profit from them.

Logotherapy, unlike other "existential" psychological movements, such as that of Binswanger, is not grounded in contemporary existential philosophy. On the other hand, it is well aware of the precepts of this philosophical stream and intends, to a degree, to correct and complement it. "Existential Analysis attempts to bring into consideration the objective correlate of decision, and the subjective correlate of knowledge, and, perhaps, in this way will be able to serve as a corrective over against existentialism."[13]

Logotherapy does not appear to be rooted in any of the modern existential philosophical systems. It is rather in the roots of this movement where basic similarities are found. Though Kierkegaard penetrated the very depths of human personality in his amazing analysis of anxiety, he nevertheless sought to stabilize this necessary subjective existence of the individual with the equally necessary counterbalance of objectivity, which he found, not in the "crowd," but rather, in God. Logotherapy, thus, is analogous as it makes an empirical analysis of basic human problems, and finds their ultimate ground not in an instinctive, dynamic organism, but rather in the One who assigns to the human being responsible tasks.

However, while Kierkegaard's analysis became psychologically dangerous in its overemphasis upon a subjectivity which sustained attentiveness on selfconscious states of experience, Frankl has emphasized that true existence is a decisive commitment away from self to the objective world of meaning and value.

---

[13] Frankl, LE, xlll.

C. *Existential Analysis and Daseinsanalysis*

Though Frankl was the first to use the term "existential analysis" (*Existenzanalyse*) to describe his psychotherapeutic research, a source of confusion has arisen in American psychological literature through the very wide use of the term to include almost any psychology which attempts to be theologically or philosophically selfconscious. The situation has been further complicated by the translation of the *Daseinsanalyse* of Ludwig Binswanger, a Swiss psychiatrist, as "existential analysis." This has sometimes led to a false identification of the theories of Frankl and Binswanger.

Binswanger attempts to understand human experience from a psychological point of view, based upon the philosophical phenomenology of Heidegger. His work has been primarily concerned with the investigation of psychotic disorders, and a demonstration of the unity of personality even in the apparently disordered "world view" of the schizophrenic. The very interesting case study of Ellen West is now widely discussed as a model of Binswanger's approach.

Daseinsanalysis is not, of course, merely the psychological explication of Heidegger's philosophy, but has, rather, many independent aspects. Frankl finds Binswanger's emphasis upon love as an existential moment a positive step beyond both Heidegger and the essentially deficient dynamic psychologies. He favorably comments that "love was placed by Ludwig Binswanger in the foreground and center of his Daseinsanalysis, and therewith, at the same time, in opposition to the Heideggerian explanation of human existence as mere 'concern' (*Sorge*)."[14]

Although Binswanger is a practising psychiatrist, Daseinsanalysis apparently does not have treatment as a central

---

[14] Frankl, LE, 76.

focus of its perspective. "The concern of Daseinsanalysis is not psychotherapeutic; at least M. Boss asserted, 'Daseinsanalysis has nothing to do with psychotherapy.' While existential analysis attempts to serve in the treatment of neuroses, the merit of Daseinsanalysis is in its contribution to the understanding of psychosis."[15] This makes a significant difference between these two schools, and Frankl rightly remarks, "Certainly Binswanger's analysis has, to a large degree, deepened and enriched our phenomenological understanding of the structure of the psychotic world view; but it is one thing to understand an illness, and another thing to treat it."[16] This is a forceful factor in the mind of the American therapist who may search in vain, among the existential psychological writings, for a theory and technique of psychotherapy. The pragmatic American will, perhaps, be more impressed with Logotherapy, if for no other reason, in the light of this distinction.

Korger and Polak, however, summarize cautionary considerations which tend to disabuse any thought that Frankl's Existential Analysis and Daseinsanalysis are essentially antagonistic. "To show the critical emphases of Existential Analysis and Daseinsanalysis as being from such different perspectives may lead to the false assumption that between these two movements stands unbridgeable opposition. This is, however, in no wise the case, for these two aspects, as anthropological directions of research, have different tasks to perform in the area of anthropology, and thus are complementary. Already the basic position of both movements — for Daseinsanalysis the understanding of psychosis, and for

---

[15] Frankl, TT, 21. The citation from Boss is taken from *Psyche*, 6, 184, 1952.
[16] Frankl, UM, 110.

Existential Analysis the treatment of neuroses – unites both
endeavors in complementary alignment."[17]

The article goes on to indicate that Existential Analysis
and Daseinsanalysis not only do not stand in each others way,
but rather, that they are joined by an "inner bond" for the
overthrow of the false psychologism of dynamic psychologies
such as that of Freud's psychoanalysis. "Presently the Daseinsanalysis of Ludwig Binswanger and the Existential Analysis of Viktor Frankl, are the greatest and most comprehensive attempts to untie themselves from the basic position of
Freud."[18]

Because this attempt is of such significance in Frankl's
works, a discussion of the logotherapeutic critique of dynamic
psychology is in order.

D. *Logotherapy and Dynamic Psychology*

Much of Frankl's literary effort has been a critique of socalled dynamic psychology. He understands dynamic psychology to be that in which a person is regarded as the result
of instinctive drives or similar organic energies. In view of
the very extensive influence of psychoanalysis, and, to a lesser
degree, Individual Psychology, in the field of psychotherapy,
he senses an urgent need to slough off the caricature of man
which is inherent in them.

Though many psychodynamically oriented therapists deny
the relevance of a philosophy of man to their "scientific" analyses, it is very obvious that every therapy has a philosophy,

---

[17] Korger, M., and Polak, P., "Der geistesgeschichtliche Ort der
Existenzanalyse": *Handbuch der Neurosenlehre und Psychotherapie*,
Urban & Schwarzenberg, Münich and Berlin, 1959, p. 641.

[18] Ibid. Cited from Matussek, *Metaphysische Probleme der Medizin.*

whether conscious or unconscious. That these underlying philosophies of man are very active in the therapeutic situation, in spite of a supposed neutrality, is noted by Gutheil: "The patients of adlerians have, apparently, only problems of power, and their conflicts appear to be exclusively conditioned by their ambition, their striving for superiority and the like. The patients of the disciples of Jung flood their physicians with archetypes and all kinds of anagogic symbolisms. The freudians hear the castration complex, the birth trauma, and similar things stated by their patients."[19]

Frankl, in spite of basic disagreements, does not deny the great contribution of his former fellow citizens of Vienna, Sigmund Freud and Alfred Adler, who introduced to our generation the psychodynamic view of man. On the contrary, he says, "Any new development in psychotherapy must necessarily be grounded on Psychoanalysis and Individual Psychology. It is our strict duty to keep these foundations in mind."[20]

He sees Freud's "pleasure principle" and Adler's "drive for social status" as complementary aspects of human functioning. Though complementary, these two foundational factors, nevertheless, still do not complete an adequate view of personality. Just as the foundation of a house needs the superstructure before it becomes a building, so must Psychoanalysis and Individual Psychology be "built up" if there is to be a concept of man adequate for psychotherapy. Frankl views this "building up" the unique task of Logotherapy. In this sense, the title, the "third Viennese school of psychiatry" signifies more than mere historical sequence.

---

[19] Frankl, MS, 79 (cited from *American Journal of Psychotherapy*, vol. II, 369, 1957).

[20] Frankl, "Religion and Existential Psychotherapy," *Gordon Review*, Vol. VI, Spring-Summer, 1960, p. 1.

Inasmuch as these dynamic psychologies presume that they are complete and independent, they become onesided and deficient. Thus the proverbial half truth becomes more dangerous than that which is completely false. This danger eventuates in the "psychologism" of dynamic psychology. Psychologism reduces every human experience to the psychological plane and thus gives a distorted view of man. Frankl often uses the following illustration to clarify this point. When one projects a sphere, a cone, and a cylinder on a plane surface, they may appear to be the same. However, this projection lacks total perspective, and thus obliterates the distinctive shape of each object. So the dynamic psychologies ignore the spiritual aspect of human nature and convert man into a mechanism of instinctive drives.

1. Psychoanalysis

According to Frankl, Freud's psychoanalysis has "sinned against" the spiritual nature of man in three ways: by depersonalizing him, by "derealizing" him, and by devaluating his scale of values.

a. Depersonalization

The depersonalization of man is not a new phenomenon, as we have already observed in the preceding chapter, but it has received a new emphasis in psychoanalysis. Here personality is regarded as the outworking of an innate dynamic force known as the "id." It is an unconscious, amoral, irrational psychic energy which is primarily sexual in nature. This sexuality is, however, to be understood in a much wider sense than genital functioning, and is practically synonymous with pleasure. Parenthetically, it may be pointed out, however, that one will search in vain in Freud's writings for a clinical illustration which is not interpreted in the conventional sense of genital sexuality.

The id operates upon this pleasure principle, and strives for the reduction of tension in the organism through pleasurable satisfactions.

However, the environment does not always provide the means for the satisfaction of this pleasure drive, for instance, not every physical object may be eaten, or every liquid drunk, or every person engaged in copulation. Therefore the human organism must develop an executive function in order to appropriate the necessary objects in the environment. This executive, the "ego," a conscious and rational eddy, emerging from the psychic stream, develops out of the id in early childhood. It seeks to meet the demands of the id in terms of a "reality principle."

The activity of the ego is complicated by the fact that not all "real," or possible, means for the reduction of tension are ideal, i.e., permissible. This is due to a third subdivision of the psychic force which operates according to an "ideal principle." This force, the "superego," is partly conscious and partly unconscious, and tends to censor the execution of the ego and the expression of the id. The superego is structured from the original psychic energy of the id by the influence of authoritative individuals upon the ego, such as parents, or, perhaps, pastors, who control to some extent the ego functions of the young child. When the child grows up and attains a relative measure of independence from these authoritative individuals, he will still be governed by the attitudes implanted earlier.

The superego has both positive and negative aspects. The positive, the ego-ideal, formed from the praise, compliments, and affirmations of the authority figures, projects an ideal of personality into the mind of the individual. The conscience, the other aspect of the superego, consists of negations, restrictions, and inhibitions that were also part of the social environment of the young child.

The balance of power of the id, ego, and superego, will determine the personality patterns of the individual. All personality patterns, as well as all personality problems, derive from the interplay of these psychic components. All personality adjustment must, likewise, come from a readjustment of these three functions of innate psychic energy.

The reader should not be beguiled by the superficial simplicity of this summary of Freud's view of personality. His theories were ever changing, and were very complex. However, this brief account will suffice to indicate the essential dynamics, and to orient the criticism of the logotherapeutic school.

As a psychological system which exhaustively accounts for the factors of human experience and personality, Frankl considers it a fantastic Munchausenian episode in which "the ego drags itself, by the forelock of the superego, out of the muck of the id."[21] Psychoanalytic concepts compose a modern mythology and they should be treated as such. It is inconceivable, to Frankl, that out of an original instinctive drive such as the id, there could arise an opposing instinctive force such as the ego. "Whoever heard of a river building its own power plant!"[22]

For such characteristics as love, altruism, esthetic appreciation, and goodness, to develop from such a "dumb" and "stupid" biological force, is more characteristic of magic or mysticism than scientific investigation. The hopeful analogies

---

[21] Frankl, UG, 86.
[22] Frankl, LE, 71.

of beautiful flowers blooming up out of the mire fails, in two respects, to gloss over the difficulty of the human flower, personality, from "blooming" out of the id. The flower seed has the potential of floral beauty already within it, which is certainly not a segment of the soil. In addition, the flower is not only "driven" by the biological interaction with the elements of the soil, but also is "drawn" by the "transcendent" sun to "rise above" the humble habitation of its roots.

The inner contradiction of the psychoanalytic concepts are less disturbing, however, than the underlying attitude toward the human being. He is denatured and degraded to a bundle of instincts, a series of reflexes. The analyst then avoids personal responsibility to his patient as he becomes a psychotechnician manipulating a psychic apparatus. "Today psychotherapeutic anthropology usually has nothing to do with a picture of true man, but rather with a picture of a man who is more or less the resultant of a parallelogram of forces, whose components are called ego, id, and superego; or as a product of instinct, inheritance, and environment. However, this product is a *homunculus* instead of a man."[23]

Not only does this view of man conceal from the therapist some of the most significant aspects of the patient and his problem, but also it may expand to the political scene and convert the human being to an expendable item in the national inventory. The recent memory of Nazi gas chambers and Chinese communes should reinforce one's memory of the dangers of depersonalization.

b. Derealization

In the same manner in which psychoanalysis makes a mere object out of a human being, it also subjectivizes his world.

[23] Frankl, MS, 109.

The important persons and things in the patient's environment are reduced to factors in the romantic mythology of
infantile adjustment. People who enter into the patient's
critical experiences are represented as nothing more than re-
creations of the oedipal phase. The equipment of his world,
such as his car, his home, his tools are mere symbols of his
oral, anal, and phallic stages of development. The human
being's struggle to interact effectively in his world is interpreted as the inevitable consequence of his toilet training!
Logotherapy regards these theses as fantasy rather than
science.

An illustration of this strange situation is presented in a
clinical case of Frankl. Herein a diplomat, who was reacting
neurotically to a vocational maladjustment due to his desire
to enter private industry and the increasing dissatisfaction
with his country's foreign policy, came for treatment. He had
been under psychoanalytic treatment for five years, and had
been continually encouraged by the analyst to stay at his
job in order to overcome the father-figure antipathy which
was represented in his relationship with his boss. "The question, whether his superior really deserved to be repudiated,
and whether it was not really recommendable for the patient
to give up his diplomatic career, to change his occupation,
was not once considered through the long years of analysis."[24]

It is interesting to note that, after only a few logotherapeutic interviews, this patient changed occupation and began to
have, for the first time, a sense of meaning in his life in place
of the former frustration. Five years later he sent an unsolic-
ited report in which he stated that he was content in his new
vocation, and had been symptom free since his appointment
at the clinic.

----

[24] Frankl, MS, 102-3.

c. Devaluation

Not only does psychoanalysis reduce the person to an objective mechanism, and his objective world to a subjective
continuation of his infantile development, but it also destroys
the values of his life, at least with respect to their objectivity,
and their truly obligative character. Thus, we understand the
concise formulation by which Frankl would include the foregoing as well as the present point:[25] Psychoanalysis objectifies
(or reifies) the subjective factor, i.e., the spiritual person;
and subjectifies (or relativizes) objective factors, i.e., objective values. One of the immediate outcomes of subjecti-
fication is the equalization, or leveling, of all values, when
only regarded in terms of the pleasure principle. "Pushpin is
as good as poetry" in the psychoanalytic world view. There
are no longer worthwhile goals in life for which to live and
die. All ethical precepts are swept away by the revelation
of "moralizing" and "rationalizing" mechanisms. Values are
no longer independent of the person. They are, rather, the
ethically relative and morally indifferent derivatives of unconscious, instinctive needs. Frankl says, "For *myself*, I am
not prepared to live for the sake of my reaction formations,
or to die for the sake of my secondary rationalizations."[26]

2. INDIVIDUAL PSYCHOLOGY

Although Adler added a necessary factor in human dynamics, and revealed the social factors in the development of
personality, according to Logotherapy, he did not escape the
psychologism basic to dynamic psychologies.

---

[25] Cf. Frankl, HP, 11-12.
[26] Frankl, MS, 104-5.

Freud had viewed the psychological process as a tight psychic causal ring modeled after the physics of his day, the law of the conservation of energy. Adler attempted to break out of this causal ring and to present man as functioning in terms of purpose. Frankl commends such an aim, but believes that Adler missed the target by regarding the psychic structure of man in terms of dynamic drive, and thus undercutting his teleology. Frankl warns against the error of confusing the "meaning of human existence" in Existential Analysis with the "life tasks" of Individual Psychology, for "in spite of all the overlapping, the life tasks are attributed, in the *vital dimension*, to instincts and in the *social dimension*, to tradition."[27] Individual Psychology, with its apparent center in teleology, nevertheless is circumscribed, in the first place, by another determinism, not a causal, but rather a final determinism; and, secondly, not a determinism in terms of instinctual, but rather in terms of social determinants. In reference to this twofold fact, Frankl says[28] that, concerning the full human phenomenon called love, Freudian psychology saw only the aspect of sexual drivenness, whereas Adlerian psychology restricted its view to the aspect of social belongingness.

The human relationships in Individual Psychology, on the surface, present a view of personality which rises high above the cold mechanical determinism of Freud, but are really, when analyzed, the result of an innate social drive. Adler sensed the need to forsake the closed psychic system of psychoanalysis, but did not, unfortunately, discover the transcendent aspects of man's nature, the spiritual dimension, upon which a true teleology could be grounded.

[27] Frankl, HP, 43.
[28] Cf. Frankl, HP, 32.

3. ANALYTICAL PSYCHOLOGY

Another European psychiatrist who has gained considerable prominence today, in spite of his rather cryptic style of writing, and the rather unorthodox areas of psychiatric research (e.g., alchemy, and oriental mysticism), is Carl Jung, whose theory is often known as Analytical Psychology.

Whereas Adler greatly reduced the area, and the importance, of the unconscious in psychological process, Jung has greatly extended it. Not only is there a personal unconscious, in the Freudian sense, but there is also a "collective unconscious" from which psychic energy flows to the individual. In this racial depository are all the experiences of mankind collected. This psychic force appears through images, symbols, or, more popularly, archetypes. The existence of the collective unconscious is substantiated, in Jung's theory, by the similarity of archetypes found in the dreams, religious symbols, and mystical experiences of human beings of diverse cultures and in different eras.

Personality development, or the process of individuation, depends upon whether the direction of the flow of psychic energy from the collective unconscious is toward the subjective person or toward the objective world (introvert or extravert), and the individual's particular mode of utilizing this energy. This latter process may be by sensing, feeling, thinking, or intuiting.

One of the most prominent of the archetypes is God, and Jung believes that nearly every adult personality problem is centered in the inability to make a satisfactory religious adjustment. For this reason Jung is often hailed as the one who truly takes into consideration the spiritual and religious factors of man. Frankl, however, sees him as falling into the same "psychodynamic" and, hence, psychologistic, error as

Freud and Adler. Religiosity and spiritual experience become just additional aspects of the instinctive libidinal drive. "According to Jung 'it' (id) is religious in me, but 'I' (ego) am not expressing faith; the id drives me to God."[29]

Jung has overlooked the essential transcendent characteristic of the religious object, and has placed God among the instincts. For Frankl, religion is nothing instinctual, but "religiosity is either existential, or it is nothing."[30] Religion is not collective, but rather, personal. When psychodynamic psychology "in the form of the teaching of C. G. Jung, again and again stresses that the ego must with the id, man with his unconscious, 'come to an understanding,' then existential analysis counters with the demand that man first of all 'come to himself!' That he come to full consciousness of the full responsibility and freedom of his ego."[31] He is amazed at the theologians who become disciples of Jung without realizing that all of their transcendent aspirations are lost in the immanence of Analytical Psychology.

In short, Jung, as well as Freud and Adler, overlooks the essential characteristic of man, his spiritual dimension, and develops but a variation of psychoanalytic psychologism. The initial promise of an adequate view of man including his spiritual life is only a "persona," a mask, which momentarily obscures the presupposition that man must be understood as a product of his instincts.

E. *The Unconscious*

Frankl does not deny the existence, or the importance, of the unconscious process in human personality, which plays such a significant role in most psychodynamic theories. He

---

[29] Frankl, UG, 97.
[30] Frankl, UG, 98.
[31] Frankl, DS, p. 100

does, however, repudiate the thesis that this is a purely instinctive sphere of activity. More important than the unconscious psychic drives is the spiritual unconscious in man. Whereas psychoanalysis attempts to bring psychic factors to consciousness, Logotherapy endeavors to make conscious the spiritual nature, and subsequent potentialities and responsibilities, of the patient.

The logotherapeutic teaching warns against possible misunderstanding of the spiritual unconscious by ascribing to it divinity, or divine attributes such as omniscience, or, on the other hand, by making it an instinctual force in the Jungian sense. This unconscious religiosity, in the normal course of events, will come to consciousness, but often becomes repressed, and, occasionally, this repression is active in neurotic etiology. A discussion of the underlying factors of this unconscious spirituality will appear in later chapters.

While no clear and distinct boundary exists between the conscious and unconscious states, Frankl believes that the id and the spiritual dimension, both of which may be unconscious, are, nonetheless, to be clearly distinguished. He believes that the popular "depth" psychology must give way to a "height" psychology in order to satisfy the phenomenological data of anthropological research. "The opposite of depth psychology is not at all a superficial psychology, but rather a height psychology."[32]

In conclusion, we may note that Logotherapy has arisen from the milieu of a philosophic tradition which asserts the unique nature of man as an existing being. According to Frankl, this existence is the ability to transcend, or oppose, oneself in decisive action.[33] By the same token, Logotherapy

---

[32] Frankl, HB, 680.
[33] Frankl, "On Logotherapy and Existential Analysis," *American Journal of Psychoanalysis,* Vol. 18, (1958), pp. 28-37.

opposes contemporary psychotherapeutic theories insofar as they fail to recognize this basic anthropological fact.

Frankl considers[34] the school of Logotherapy to have a field of operation much broader than clinical psychotherapy. It circumscribes the explication of personal existence in its anthropological analysis; serves as a nonspecific psychotherapeutic method; presents itself as the specific therapeutic procedure for neuroses rooted in the spiritual dimension; is a therapy for the paraclinical "collective neuroses"; and, finally, provides to the field of medicine a much needed "medical ministry" (*Aerztliche Seelsorge*). Later chapters will discuss in detail these areas of logotherapeutic application.

We shall now turn to the view of man which serves as the foundation of the school of Logotherapy.

---

[34] "Indikationen der existenzanalytischen Logotherapie," *Wiener Archiv für Psychologie, Psychiatrie, und Neurologie*, Vol. 5, no. 3, Sept. 1955.

CHAPTER III

LOGOTHERAPY AND MAN

Logotherapy is grounded in anthropology. Its view of man is an endeavor to present a conceptual understanding of human nature which will satisfy both the empirical data of psychiatric research, and the theoretical needs of mental health. Only when one clearly understands the nature of the person behind the neurotic symptoms can he really understand those symptoms, and effectively deal with the patient manifesting them. Only when one understands fully what is entailed in the term, "human being" (or, perhaps better, "being human") can he effectively fulfill his role as a therapist. Frankl seeks to complement and "fill out" the truncated picture of man presented in most of the contemporary psychological literature and, thus, to arrive at a comprehensive view of man, adequate for the field of psychotherapy.

The initial anthropological problem is reminiscent of the ancient philosophical problem of the One and the Many. How can one maintain the unity of personality and, at the same time, do justice to its diversity? Frankl is adamant in maintaining both the unity and wholeness of man. The individual is truly *individuum* and is not subject to compartmentalization, nor reduction to an aggregate, in order to fit some "bundle hypothesis." In addition, man is not "summable," for he is complete in himself and cannot be other than figuratively construed as an integer of a larger whole. He is not an organic cell of some national psyche, as was postulated in the national socialism of Germany, nor is he an organic part of some platonic, or holistic, "world soul." "There is no 'people's soul' (*Volksseele*), not even a 'group psyche,' and insofar as the expression, 'group psychology' (LeBon), means something of this sort, this psychology, in the true sense of the word, has no object."[1]

However, Frankl is also convinced of the necessity of making provision for the rich diversity of human personality. Though he sees the value of the emphasis in the Daseinsanalysis of Binswanger upon the unity of the individual, whether in sickness or in health, he also sees a need to complement this emphasis by pointing out the fact of the essential multiplicity of man.

A. *Dimensional Ontology*

In order to avoid any disintegrating pluralism, such as is found in Cartesian body-mind dualism, Frankl has developed what he refers to as "dimensional ontology." In this, the distinctive aspects of man are not viewed as separate elements, but rather, as dimensions, or facets, of the individual. He compares this to a projection of a drinking glass which may be viewed dimensionally from one perspective as a circle, or from another as a rectangle, but which must not be

---

[1] Frankl, UM, 67.

presumed to be the result of combining these two figures. Rectangularity and circularity are obviously characteristics of the drinking glass, but, just as obviously, do not exhaust its attributes, nor constitute its unity. Frankl believes that such a dimensional approach will serve to obviate the "body-mind problem," while it does justice both to the unity and diversity of the individual.

In Logotherapy, the individual is comprised of three factors: the physical, the psychological, and the spiritual. It is emphasized that they, though having distinctive characteristics, are merely dimensional functions of man as an individual, and must not be taken as either distinct levels (Hartmann), or as concentric components (Scheler), both of which seem to lead to a commitment to an essential trichotomy.

1. BODY

The body is a material structure consisting in an organic unity of systems, such as the nervous, the endocrine, the respiratory, the circulatory, etc., which cooperate in the maintenance of the metabolic process through growth and development, and subsequent maturity and senescence. Any particular human body is the result of genetic and environmental influences.

The body of man is the result of the biological evolutionary process, It is distinct from the higher animals in its enormously complex nervous system, which enables the body to correlate with the complex symbolic functions of the spiritual dimension. Frankl believes that the "genus" man arrived when a mutation supplied the organism with 14 billion neurons (following Economo's theory of "progressive cerebration" and E. Dubois' conclusion that the ganglion cells of anthropoids, anthropids, and later hominids are in the proportion: $3\frac{1}{2}: 7: 14$) — "with that mutation, in which the hominid suddenly 'received' 14 billion neurons, can we thus date this incomplete development of man, or, if you will, the emergence of the sixth day of creation!"[2]

2. PSYCHE

The psychological character of man is derived from a system of innate drives. Frankl does not develop a theory of this psychic system in detail, but rather, presumes that this has been done sufficiently by others, and it is, instead, his task to counterbalance the onesidedness which has resulted from an overemphasis upon these drives. He believes that the observations of Freud, Adler, and Jung have thrown considerable light upon the psychic process of man, and have provided some very useful information. They must not, however, be allowed to obliterate, or to misinterpret, data from the spiritual experiences of the individual.

The psyche is constantly changing throughout developmental stages, and the subsequent habit pattern formations and changes. The decisive activities of the past become part of the automatic influences of the present. The ego of today, as Berze says, becomes the id of tomorrow; or as Frankl interprets it: the decisions of today become the drives of tomorrow.

3. PSYCHOPHYSICUM

The body and psyche are closely coordinated in the logotherapeutic theory and are designated together as the "psychophysicum." These two dimensions consist of inherited characteristics and function automatically. They are not interactive inasmuch as their functions are qualitatively different and, hence, not deducible to a common factor. They

---

[2] Frankl, UM, 39.

are, rather, presented as co-functioning in a manner that reminds one of the socalled "psycho-physical parallelism" of Spinoza. This latter phrase is, as a matter of fact, sometimes used in Logotherapy to describe the activity of the psychophysicum.

Frankl repudiates the behavioristic reduction of the psychophysicum to a materialistic monism on both empirical and philosophical grounds,[3] whether in terms of a crude "watsonian" identification, or the disposing of psychic process to a mere epiphenomenal status. A presently felt hunger pang may well be conditioned by tissue needs and/or peristaltic stomach activity, but it is certainly not the tissue condition itself.

The dimensional ontology of Logotherapy may be pictured as a two dimensional, rather clearly defined, horizontal base, the psychophysicum, with the spirit, as the vertical dimension, rising to indefinite heights.

Frankl likens the body to a piano, while the psyche is represented by the pianist, who can "activate" the piano, and the spiritual dimension, in turn, is represented by the artistic "necessity" of the pianist. "The physical makes possible the psychological activation of a spiritual demand."[4] The three dimensions are readily observable in a case of hyperthyroidism. The somatic factor, the glandular disturbance, is accompanied by the psychic state of, perhaps, agoraphobia, or an intense anxiety state. The spiritual is revealed in the attitude of the person in question to his psychophysical condition.

4. SPIRIT

In the logotherapeutic theory of man, it is the spiritual dimension which is of central importance. It is the spiritual

---

[3] Cf. Frankl, UM, 41 ff.
[4] Frankl, UM, 60.

which truly constitutes the person. While it is proper to say that one *has* a psyche, or a body, he must say that he *is* a spiritual being. This must not be misconstrued as spiritualism, the converse of materialistic monism or psychologism, for the psychophysicum, though not primary, is yet a very necessary dimensional factor in man. "Thus not only in the 'third' dimension, that of the spiritual, but rather, first in the tri-dimensionality of body, psyche, and spirit: first in this tri-unity is *homo humanus* 'at home.'"[5] Some have failed to appreciate this distinction and have accused Frankl of falling into the "spiritualistic fallacy" of disregarding the material factors of man. This is certainly easy to gainsay inasmuch as Frankl is a competent neurologist, has developed a tranquilizing medication, and is continually searching for possible somatic factors that may underlie neurotic disorders!

The personality of man is the phenomenology of the spirit. It is the spiritual as it is revealed through the psychophysicum, which serves as both an expression of the spirit, and an instrument for its activity. The spiritual-noetic dimension itself is, in turn, revealed through the existentiality of the spirit. "The three constituents of human existence: spirituality, freedom, and responsibility, represent irreducible and indeducible phenomena of humanity; they are original phenomena (*Urphaenomene*) and no epiphenomena."[6] These "existentials" are neither analyzable nor synthesizable — they are just there (*Dasein*).

B. *Basic Human Characteristics*

1. SPIRITUALITY

Spirituality is derived from what, in Logotherapy, is called the "spiritual unconscious." "Unconscious spirituality is the

---

[5] Frankl, HB, 670.
[6] Frankl, MS, 99.

origin and root of all consciousness. In other words, we know and acknowledge, not only an instinctive unconscious, but rather, also a *spiritual unconscious,* and in it we see the supporting ground of all conscious spirituality. The ego is not *governed by the id;* but the spirit is *borne by the unconscious.*"[7]

Spirituality is not discovered empirically, but instead, phenomenologically. It is revealed initially in immediate self-consciousness, and then in the conceptual ability of man, in his symbolic-linguistic faculty, as well as in his reflective selfconsciousness. It is the chief attribute of man.

From the spiritual unconscious, according to Frankl,[8] the following three intuitive moments emerge: conscience, by which ethical necessities which pertain to the individual personality and his concrete situation, and thus elude generalization, are conceived; love, by which the unique possibilities of the beloved personality are grasped; and esthetic conscience, by which artistic achievements are guided. These are essentially emotional, and nonrational functions, and can only be rationalized in retrospect. "Unconscious," in reference to the spiritual dimension, always refers to the impossibility of self reflection. Forced attempts at self reflection of these intuitive moments thus bring only frustration.

The spirit is essentially unconscious, in this respect, inasmuch as it can not be objectified and analyzed. "Just as the point of origin of the retina, namely, the entrance of the optic nerve, is a 'blind spot' on the retina, so is it with the spirit, which is, as to its origin, blind to all self observation and self reflection."[9] Thus the spirit itself must be known "by its fruit."

---

[7] Frankl, HB, 674.
[8] Frankl, HB, 675-6.
[9] Frankl, UG, 33-4.

It is the spiritual dimension that distinguishes man from the animals. In a real sense, animals *are* their biological and instinctive drives, whereas man merely *has* them. This is a most important distinction for the discipline of psychotherapy.

Since the spiritual is not a materialistic entity, it may be difficult for those reared in a behavioristic generation to comprehend the relationship between the spiritual and the psychophysicum. The spiritual is neither inside nor outside the body, for spatial characteristics are not applicable. Frankl asserts that the spiritual is "with" (*Bei-sein*) other objects and persons in the world. Through this spiritual dimension man can, in a real sense, be with a distant, or departed, loved one. This faculty of the spirit is that by which man is enabled to have a trans-spatial and trans-temporal reference epistemologically. Hereby he knows not only himself, but also other things and persons.

Traditional epistemology tended to divorce the subject and object of knowledge, and, thereby, to eventuate in a skepticism about the "outside" world. Frankl believes that "we must unconditionally backtrack to a place prior to the separation of this relationship (*Dasein*) into subject and object."[10] Epistemological theories have "onticized," or separated into "things," this ontological relationship. Frankl also warns against the radical retreat of some contemporary philosophers, however, who have declared that they have "overcome" the ontological rift between the subject and object (even Heidegger, the leading spirit of existential philosophy does not claim this).

In Logotherapy, the traditional distinction is maintained, but the subject is not removed from its ontological relation-

---

[10] Frankl, HB, 673.

ship to the world of objects. "The subject by its cognitive acts is capable of approaching the object, and, thereby, establishing that cognitive closeness to the things in the world which I have called 'being with' (Bei-sein) the object."[11] The wonder of cognition is this attainment of the object, which, however, still remains an object.

In addition to the cognizing power of the spiritual dimension, in Logotherapy, the reality of the objective world is firmly asserted. "Any philosophy or psychology which, by its careful investigation of the psychic phenomena in their richness and fullness, deserves to be called a 'phenomenological approach,' must acknowledge the primordial fact that every true cognitive act implies the objectivity of the object."[12] Man can grasp only a subjective segment of this world, but it is, nonetheless, an objective order from which he "cuts out" this segment.

The spirit is not always immediately "visible," nor effective in human personality. In mental defects, psychotic personalities, and infants, this spirituality may be hidden, except for careful observation. Only a "glorified" psychophysicum could fully express the existentiality of the spirit, which is also obscured in neurotic existence. However, ordinarily, it may be readily observed, when one is not committed to a view of man which posits the non-existence of spirituality, and thus excludes apriori this essentially, and essential, human data.

The spiritual dimension is most fully revealed in man's existentiality, through his freedom, and in his transcendence, by his responsibility. We shall turn now to these two existentials.

---

[11] Frankl, "Beyond Self-Actualization and Self-Expression," Journal of Existential Psychiatry, Vol. 1, No. 1, Spring 1960.
[12] Idem.

2. FREEDOM

Freedom is the ground for man's special modes of existence which are distinctive of his species and separate him from the animals. It is the most immediate fact of his awareness. His personality is determined by his free choices; man is a "deciding creature" (Jaspers). "But what *is* man? He is the essence which always decides. And he again and again decides what he will be in the next instant."[13] Only man is able, in this sense, to choose himself, to exist.

In the first place, man is free from his instinctive drives. Just as he has the ability to affirm these psychic impulses, so does he have the power to deny them. He is also free from his inherited characteristics. Although he is conditioned by the limits set by his genetic structure, yet is he unconditioned as to what he will do within these limits. Frankl cites the case[14] of identical twins who had a high intelligence factor. However, one of them became a clever criminal and the other an equally clever criminologist. In the third place, man is also free from his environment. Though an economically depressed area may, in some cases, tend to engender delinquent attitudes, it also may provide a springboard, for social leadership to eradicate the slums, for that free man who decides to overcome his environmental pressures.

It must not be supposed that man must always strive with these conditioning factors, for, fortunately, in many, if not most, of his experiences, his faculty of freedom cooperates with his drives, inherited characteristics, and environmental circumstances. Nevertheless, it should be ever present in mind that he is free, if he will to be, from these conditioning factors. In this sense, man is an unconditioned being.

---

13 Frankl, LE, 7.
14 Frankl, HB, 682.

Unfortunately, in some instances this aspect of man's existential freedom has been overemphasized, especially in the French existentialism as propounded by Sartre (noted also in the preceding chapter). Herein freedom has been presented as the exclusive attribute of personality, and, thus, man appears to create both himself and his world from his own subjective milieu. Frankl, however, insists that freedom is not only *from* something, but that, in addition, and most importantly, is freedom *for* something. This brings us to the third existential attribute of man, according to Logotherapy: responsibility.

3. RESPONSIBILITY

Freedom must not be identified with omnipotence or arbitrariness, for man is only conditionally unconditioned. Not only is man's freedom restricted by the limits of his psychophysicum, and his context in the world, but he is also free only insofar as he fulfills his freedom *to* responsibility. In freedom is revealed man's existentiality, while in responsibility his transcendence is revealed.[15] He is responsible to actualize and realize meaning and values in an objective world replete with tasks and opportunities. What he does should not be dictated by his own arbitrary choice, but rather, is a transcendent assignment. "Responsibility can only come to us from a higher court than ourselves. If we derive the ego from the id (the will from the instincts) and trace back the superego to the ego (moral obligation to the will), then we gain no correct view, but rather, a caricature of man."[16]

Frankl sees the ground of this responsibility in the phenomenon of conscience. He repudiates the psychodynamic view

---

[15] Cf. Frankl, HB, 686 ff.
[16] Frankl, TT, 158.

of conscience as developing out of unconscious psychic libido, and asserts the voice of conscience to be an inexorable "thou shalt," spontaneously appearing to man's consciousness out of the depth (or, perhaps one should say, the height) of the spiritual unconscious. Conscience is immediate, intuitive and absolute. It is basically unconscious and non-rational, according to Logotherapy. It is non-rational because it is pre-logical, that is to say, it is prior to any rational reflection. It is not a universal moral law in the sense of the Kantian imperative, however, but rather, an individual moral law, coming to light in a concrete situation of a specific person. It is, nonetheless, imperative, however, because it is a transcendent moment. "Every categorical imperative receives its legitimation exclusively from transcendence, but not from immanence."[17]

Conscience, though not a universal moral law, is nevertheless, universal, and the irreligious man also has a conscience and responsibility, both of which he fails to appreciate. He convinces himself that his conscience is a mere psychological product within him, which he may, therefore, disregard, inasmuch as he is only responsible to himself to obey it. The unbeliever fails to inquire further as to conscience and responsibility which would lead him to transcendence.

This responsibility before the conscience leads to the question as to whether there is someone behind the conscience to give it moral sanction and objectivity. "In the final analysis it must certainly appear questionable whether man could really be responsible before something — or whether responsibility is only possible when it is before someone."[18] Frankl posits as the only plausible ground for the conscience, a personal structure, a *personalissimum* — God. "Behind the

---

[17] Frankl, UG, 83.
[18] Frankl, HB, 694.

superego of man stands 'thou God,' the conscience is the 'thou word' of transcendence."[19] He avoids referring to this transcendent ground of objective reality as "it," or even "he," inasmuch as these categories may have no relevance to a transcendent Being. "All declarations pertaining to God are only valid by analogy. Likewise also is every assertion pertaining to his personality: he is quasi-personal, is a Superperson."[20]

In Logotherapy, God is not psychologized away as a projection of a father image, but rather, Frankl sees the father as the first concrete image which the child has of God. "Only ontogenetically, biologically, and biographically is the father first, ontologically, however, God is the first."[21]

Neither does Logotherapy take recourse to psychic archetypes as an explanation for God. Frankl considers this a reduction of God to a mere moral instinct, whereas our basic conception of God is not based upon primitive forms of the collective unconscious, but rather, upon God Himself, and the personal decision of man for, or against, Him. Man is responsible, as a basic dimension of his personality, because he must "respond" to the "call" of God.

When man, confronted by the transcendence behind the voice of conscience, ponders the nature of transcendent reality, he must beware of the ever lurking dangers of "anthropocentrism" and "anthropomorphism."[22] In anthropocentrism, man is idolized, and set up as the standard, both of meaning and value. This is futile for "man cannot possibly be his own yardstick. He can measure himself only by the Absolute, by an absolute value, by God."[23] Anthropomorphism is, con-

[19] Frankl, UG, 85.
[20] Frankl, HP, 106.
[21] Frankl, HB, 695.
[22] Cf. Frankl, HP, 80 ff.
[23] Frankl, HP, 96.

versely, the error of regarding God as "made in man's image," a projection of human personality. Though man is truly an image of God, he can only be asymptotically compared to the "original." Frankl believes that the essential distinction of immanence and transcendence in anthropological phenomena must be carefully maintained.

The existential analysis of man, according to Logotherapy, may, thus, be presented in three developmental phases: Man is discovered by a phenomenological analysis to be a being having responsibility; the analysis then discloses a spiritual, as well as a psychic unconscious, which, as conscience, is the ground for responsibility; and in the third developmental phase is revealed the religious transcendence — the "unconscious God."[24]

This analysis puts religious concepts at the very center of anthropology and restores the spiritual functions of man to their appropriate significant place. It is an unapologetic thesis of Logotherapy that man can only be fully understood in the light of a supernatural reality. "Today we do not rack our brains anymore over the 'future of an illusion'; but we think a good deal about the 'eternity of a reality' — over the eternity and presence, the omnipresence of that Reality, which has been unveiled in the religiosity of man."[25]

C. Developmental Problems

In a view of man in which mature existential decisions play a major role, the question arises as to the status of those members of the species which are incapable of manifesting responsible freedom, such as children and mental defectives.

[24] This is the title and theme of one of Frankl's books: *Der unbewusste Gott.* Cf. Bibliography.
[25] Frankl, UG, 103.

Though persons in these categories fail to be authentic persons in the strict sense of the word, inasmuch as their sense of responsibility either cannot be, or, at least, has not yet been, brought to consciousness; yet they have, potentially, all the characteristics of the existential human being. Frankl likens these situations to an airplane, which is still an airplane while taxiing on the ground, but which becomes truly an airplane when it takes to the air.

It is also to be noted that the "hidden" person behind these instances of incomplete development may often be revealed, when one brings attention to the persons themselves rather than to adult standards of comparison. In both normal and special education, there has been amazing progress made when the emotional and spiritual spheres are areas of tuition, rather than, exclusively, the traditional rational process.

Frankl discusses the plight of idiocy in reference to the possibility of moral decisions, and true existence, through inner attitudes, and affirms such possibilities: "Only God can know how many saints were concealed behind the miens of idiots."[26] He believes that any attempt to measure authentic existence in terms IQ is really intellectual conceit. "I can conceive that the fact of idiocy itself, or how one adjusts to the fact that he is 'imprisoned' by an inferior brain, can be the occasion, or even the opportunity, for a task, the mastery of which provides a most significant achievement of value."[27]

D. *Motivation*

One of the most distinctive aspects of Logotherapy is its theory of human motivation. Frankl repudiates the home-

---

[26] Frankl, "Collective Neuroses of the Present Day," *Internationales Journal für prophylaktische Medizin und Sozialhygiene*, June 1958, p. 4.

[27] Frankl, TT, 16.

ostasis principle of biology as the motivating force in personality. He believes that no theory based upon a reduction of tension, or a satisfaction of psycho-biological drives, can adequately account for human action. It is even doubtful if such a point of view is valid even in the exclusively biological realm.[28]

Frankl considers the psychoanalytic pleasure principle a self contradicting thesis, for the intention of pleasure, as the goal of activity, obviates the pleasure as a consequence. Thus, if the pleasure principle is ever descriptive of human motivation, it is so only in cases of personality problems.

By the same token, the contemporary attempt to confine the motivational impulses to some form of self-expression, self-fulfillment, or self-actualization, is inadequate. Such an attempt leads to the same dilemma as the foregoing hedonistic view, for, insofar as man sets as his goal the realization of himself, he is, to that degree, unable to attain that goal. The inherent self-reflection in such theories is a hindrance to actualization. Think of the poor public speaker when he begins to reflect upon how he is speaking!

Self-reflection is usually the result of a failure in the performance of some task. It is like a boomerang, often erroneously presumed to have return flight as its essential purpose, which returns to the hunter only when it has missed the prey.[29]

A vague self-fulfillment, as well as other self regarding motives, such as pleasure, happiness, morality, or tranquility, are self defeating, for these experiences are to be attained as

---

[28] Cf. C. Bühler, "Theoretical Observations about Life's Basic Tendencies," *American Journal of Psychotherapy,* July 1959, pp. 561-581.

[29] Cf. Frankl, "Existential Analysis and Logotherapy," Paper read at the Fourth International Congress at Barcelona, Spain, Sept. 1958, p. 5.

effects rather than being intentions. "Only when the primary objective orientation is lacking and has foundered, does that interest in one's self arise, as it is so strikingly manifested in neurotic existence. Therefore the striving for self-fulfillment is in no way something primary, rather, we see in it a deficient mode, and a reduced level of human existence."[30]

The point of view which holds that man's central motive is the attainment of social status, reminiscent of Adler's Individual Psychology, is also repudiated by Frankl. He construes this as just another aspect of self-reflection, inherently destructive of successful activity. Actually, the way one truly attains social status is not by aiming to do so, but, conversely, by disregarding one's self, and seeking to better the social status of the other person. The more one strives for prestige, instead of achievement, the less one will succeed.[31]

The primary motivation, in logotherapeutic teachings, is that which is directed toward meaning and values. Appropriate human striving is that which is directed toward objectively meaningful tasks, whether in reference to objects, other persons, or God. Frankl believes that one of the most serious problems of contemporary society is the lack of such meaningful life experiences.

Modern man can find no meaning in life. Such a situation is called, in Logotherapy, "existential frustration." Sheer activity may sometimes narcotize an individual and, thus, to some extent obscure this meaninglessness, but even this possibility is diminishing due to the great increase of leisure time and the transitory attraction of irrelevant hobbies. The increase of relaxation from the pressure of work, which has been a long sought social goal, seems only to increase this

---

[30] Frankl, "Logotherapie und Existenzanalyse," Paper read at the International Congress of Psychotherapy, Barcelona, 1958, p. 6.
[31] Cf. Frankl, HP, 22.

phenomenon of existential frustration, or, as it is sometimes, in Logotherapy, called, "existential vacuum." This existential vacuum is not pathogenic *per se;* however, it often is the ground for neurotic problems and, in addition, is a situation in which neuroses stemming from a somatic or a psychic condition may abound.

Thus Frankl considers the realization of objective meaning and values the true motivational foundation of man. Only the person who decisively sets himself to a purposeful task fulfills himself and his true end, and avoids those psychic conflicts inherent in all striving based upon self regard.

In Logotherapy, three types of values are presented, which may properly serve as the ends of human endeavor: creative values, such as those in which an individual creates a work of art or fulfills a vocational task; experiential values, which may derive from an emotional situation, such as a love relationship, or an esthetic experience, such as the observation of a beautiful sunset; and, finally, attitudinal values, which may be evidenced in the willingness to accept a difficult circumstance, an extreme case of which might be the necessary suffering of an inoperable cancer.

The "will to meaning," therefore, in Logotherapy, is the true motivational factor in authentic human existence, while the realizing of values is the true responsibility of man. The range of value potentialities is evaluated by an objective moral order revealed through the conscience, and expressive of the will of God. Apart from such a qualification, the creative, and possibly esthetic, experience involved in the production of lamp shades from human skin would be on par with the alleviation of the distress of a person in danger. Frankl does not attempt to set forth a specific axiological system, but rather, presumes that this is revealed to each individual in his spiritual dimension, except, perhaps, in those cases where this "individual moral law" of conscience has been effectively repressed into the unconscious.

E. *The Person*

In Logotherapy it is emphasized that man is a person, rather than a reflex mechanism, or a mere biological specimen. Frankl develops this concept in a summary fashion in his book *Logos und Existenz* (ch. 2) in terms of ten theses characterizing the person:

1. The person is an individual. Man is an indivisible unity, even in extreme situations, such as schizophrenia, or alternating personality. All personality theories must be grounded in this fact.

2. A person is complete in himself. Man must not be construed as an organic segment of some higher personal unit, such as a race, a social group, or a national entity. Even in procreation there is no divisibility or fusibility, for it is only the organism that is reproduced, and not the person.

3. A person is an absolute novelty. Each man is a creation of God. "The father is in no way the creator (*Zeuger*) of his child, but rather a mere witness (*Zeuge*) of the miracle, that always occurs with the advent of a new human being, a new person."[32]

4. A person is spiritual. The psychophysical organism is of great importance, but only as the instrument and expression of the real person, manifest through the spiritual dimension. The organism, as a tool, has great *utility*, but the person has *worth*, which is independent of all vital and social usefulness.

5. A person is existential. Man is a faculty, rather than a fact, and decides, from among the possibilities presented to

[32] Frankl, LE, 51.

him, what he will be. "A human being is, as Jaspers has designated, a 'deciding' being: he decides at any given moment, what he will, in the next moment, be."[33]

6. A person is an *ego* and not an *id*. Man is not propelled by an unconscious instinctive force, but rather empowered by a spiritual unconscious. Herein are his faith and his religious aspirations grounded. However, when one does come to God, Frankl firmly believes that it must be by *decision*, and not by having been *driven*, even if by a socalled "spiritual" force. "Religiosity is either spontaneous decision, or it is nothing at all."[34]

7. A person is not only a unity (1) and complete in himself (2), but he also establishes unity and completeness in the physical-psychological-spiritual unity which describes the totality of man. During lifetime, these dimensions are not separable. They are neither levels, or layers, but rather man is, as it were, the intersection of these three modes of being.

8. A person is dynamic. He is not to be hypostatized as a static substance, but is, rather, an unfolding, active existence. Man is ever a process of Becoming.

9. An animal is not a person. Animals are not able to transcend themselves, nor to oppose themselves in existential decision. They have no world (*Welt*), only an environment (*Umwelt*). Frankl believes that animals are analogously related to man, as man, in turn, is related to God. Thus God is, at least, a person, and, to be sure, a Superperson, about whom we must speak only by analogy.

10. A person can only be understood, when viewed as being in the image of God. Man can only properly conceive of himself in the light of transcendence, especially through

---

[33] Frankl, LE, 56-57.
[34] Frankl, LE, 60.

the voice of transcendence in his conscience. "The conscience is the communications center of transcendence."[35]

The foregoing anthropology is the heart of the logotherapeutic theory. Every illness is understood, and every therapeutic method is applied, in reference to it. As a psychiatrically oriented system, Logotherapy has, of course, a primary concern for those persons who have foundered in the sea of emotional instability, and are desperately struggling to reach the haven of good health. The analysis of such human disturbances is the occupation of the succeeding chapter.

---

[35] Frankl, LE, 64.

CHAPTER IV

LOGOTHERAPY
AND MENTAL ILLNESS

Although Logotherapy is initially interested in an adequate view of man, this resulting anthropological perspective is considered specifically with respect to the field of mental health. It is a psychiatric view of man.

A. *Diagnosis*

Frankl considers the proper diagnosis of mental illness the first, and one of the most important, step in psychotherapy. He paraphrases the classic statement: *Qui bene distinguit, bene docet* (who distinguishes well, teaches well) by substituting *bene curat* (cures well). He acknowledges the difficulty involved in proper diagnostic procedures, however, in view of the intimate relationships of the dimensions of personality. Inasmuch as every human experience is a total experience, and involves the whole man, one should not be surprised to find this also to be the case in pathological circumstances.

In Logotherapy, it is considered of prime importance to discover the primary cause of a state of illness, as opposed to the secondary causal factor, which is usually negligible as far as the diagnosis is concerned. The aim is not to determine any proportional etiology, but rather, only to bring to light the most significant casual factor, or, on occasion, factors.

Only by such a procedure does Frankl believe that a purposeful therapy can be utilized. Because there are invariably somatic factors, which must be taken into account in the diagnostic procedure, he believes that psychotherapy is primarily the province of the psychiatrically trained physician.

Inasmuch as a physical factor may be the cause of a malfunctioning in the psychic dimension, and vice versa, it may appear that diagnosis will lead one to the old conundrum: which came first, the chicken or the egg? However, such theoretical problems are quickly dispersed in a real life situation. Frankl says, confronted with a real hen and a real egg, it is relatively easy to determine which came first!

Because there is a time factor involved in the causal sequence between these two dimensions, the relationship must be represented as a spiral, rather than a merely circular reciprocation of the physical and the psychological.

The situation is, of course, further complicated by the third dimension, the spiritual, which is also present in every human experience. In the Foreword to his *Theorie und Therapie der Neurosen*, Frankl clearly sets forth this complication: "Every theory and therapy of neurosis moves upward on a ladder which stands upon a clinical ground, and reaches upward to a meta-clinical space. From heuristic grounds, and for didactic purposes, it must be presented as though we had distinct rungs in this 'Jacob's Ladder,' but there are really no pure somatogenic, psychogenic, or noogenic neuroses. There are merely mixed cases, cases in which, respectively, a somatogenic, psychogenic, or noogenic moment moves into the foreground of the theoretical object, and the therapeutic objective. Such a *reservatio mentalis* is to be read between the lines."

Frankl believes that diagnosis should not be *per exclusionem,* for he has discovered that when the diagnosis is made in deference to psychic factors, merely on the basis of a negative physical examination (and in spite of the insufficient evidence), subsequently significant physical etiological factors may be revealed. Thus a diagnosis should always be positive.

Frankl is somewhat skeptical concerning the use of psycho-diagnostic testing instruments and procedures in the diagnosis of mental illnesses.[1] In cases where the symptomatology is clear, there is no need for such tests, and where the diagnosis is very difficult, or borderline, the tests are not sensitive enough to be reliable. He does not deny that psychological diagnostic test research is valid for personality study, but finds it of dubious value in psychotherapeutic practice. In addition, such tests tend to "type" individuals in such a way that they may cover over the essential uniqueness of the individual.[2]

Proper diagnosis can only be carried out when undergirded by a clear theoretical foundation. To this task, Frankl has, through the years, devoted a great deal of time and energy. He sets forth a general outline of pathology based upon two factors: the etiological, or genetic factor; and the phenomenological, or symptomatic factor. These two factors are, in

---

[1] Cf. Frankl, "Kann man die Seele messen und wägen?", *Neue Volksbildung,* Austrian Ministry of Education, 8, 1957, p. 24.

[2] Cf. Frankl, AS, 57, 58.

turn, related to two personality dimensions, the psychic, and the somatic.

		SYMPTOMATOLOGY	
		psychic	somatic
ETIOLOGY	somatic	PSYCHOSIS	COMMON DISEASES
	psychic	NEUROSIS	ORGAN NEUROSIS

B. *Psychosis*

A psychosis is defined by Frankl as a pathological situation in which there is a somatic etiology, and a psychic symptomatology. It is somewhat characteristic of European psychiatry, as opposed to the popular distinction of functional psychoses on the American scene, to posit a physical basis for psychosis, in spite of the absence of positive evidence. "It is, naturally, not said hereby that the supposed somatic causes of psychosis have already been scientifically elucidated."[3] Frankl, however, shoulders the "scandal of psychiatry" (K. Schneider) and refers to the socalled functional psychoses as having "cryptosomatic" causes.

It would seem, perhaps, that the more scientific procedure would be to withhold judgment as to the causation of such illnesses until positive evidence were at hand (also more in line with Frankl's diagnostic axioms). Frankl, however, makes such a decision on the basis of the lack of psychological factors, the impotence of psychological treatment

---

[3] Frankl, TT, 2.

methods in such cases, and the relative success of physical procedures in therapy.

It is especially important to diagnose properly psychotic, or endogenous depression in view of the fact that the possibility of suicide plays such a significant, and dangerous, role. Frankl has, through a long clinical experience of dealing with depressive patients, developed a simple, yet very effective, diagnostic method for such cases of depression. The imminence of suicidal intentions, or the absence of such, is what must be determined.

Inasmuch as it is sometimes erroneously reported that logotherapists challenge persons who are contemplating suicidal attempts to do so, this procedure, perhaps, should be briefly set forth here.

The patient is asked two questions, the first of which is: Are you planning to commit suicide? The answer is invariably negative, for if the patient truly has no such intention, he will say so, and if he is merely dissimulating his real intentions, he will also deny them. The second question is designed to catch the dissimulating patient off guard, and so identify him: Why not? The patient who has answered truthfully will have an answer ready at hand. He may assert his responsibility to himself, to his family, to his vocation, or, perhaps, to his church. On the other hand, the patient who is trying to deceive, in order to avoid the thwarting of his plans, or perhaps to obtain a discharge from hospitalization, will have no such ready answer.

It should be kept in mind that this diagnosis is in reference to the prevention of suicidal attempts, and should not be confused with the situations in which there are only obsessive neurotic ideas of suicide, for which a special method of treatment is presented in Logotherapy. This method will be detailed in the following chapter.

Though psychoses are defined as having a somatic causal factor, it does not follow that psychotherapy may not be sometimes helpful. This is due to the fact that the psychosis is often "overlaid" by secondary psychogenetic factors, for which psychotherapy is the indicated therapy. In addition, it is also true that the human personality appears to be somewhat self regulating, or readjusting, in one dimension when "balance" is established in another. Therefore psychotherapy, in the strict sense of the term, is, in the logotherapeutic perspective, always an indirect method of treatment for psychoses, which may be sometimes indicated in such "cryptosomatic" illnesses, such as schizophrenia and endogenous depression (manic-depression).

C. Banal Disease

Common illnesses, or, as Frankl refers to them, banal diseases, are those in which both the etiology and the symptomatology are physical. This is, therefore, not within the province of the psychiatrist, or psychotherapist, per se, except in those cases in which a psychosomatic factor is involved.

A psychosomatic disease, according to Frankl, is one, with appropriate physical pathology, but which has been precipitated by psychological factors. "Diseases which are not really caused by the psychic, but rather, merely precipitated; we designate as psychosomatic."[4] The psychic process, in some cases, for instance, lowers the level of immunity of the individual, and thus serves as a conditioning factor for the illness. The specific "choice" of the organ involved may be due to an inherited "organ inferiority" (Adler), or it may have some symbolic function relating to the precipitating psychic problem. In any respect, however, the disease in

---

[4] Frankl, HB, 720.

itself is a physiological process. Once again, psychotherapy is indicated only in reference to the amelioration of the precipitating psychic factor.

Frankl warns against the contemporary psychosomatic *Zeitgeist* in which there is a tendency to base every illness upon psychic factors. He finds this particularly prevalent in America, and specifically criticizes the usage of statistical evaluations of clinical surveys, and the widespread adherence to psychological test results, as the confirming evidence. In addition, he finds the more primitive psychoanalytic explanation for a large range of common diseases to be "tragicomical." Almost every type of illness has been set forth as grounded either in oral, anal, or phallic stages of development, castration complexes of the oedipal situation, or upon the death instinct. Such psychologism will serve only to hinder progress in the field of mental health and psychotherapy.

On the other hand, Frankl feels that the tendency in Europe, especially in Germany, with respect to psychosomatic medicine, is to be "noologistic," rather than psychologistic. Herein the disease involved is considered the expression of the spiritual dimension of man, a biographical explication. However, the psychophysicum, as the means, or instrument, and the expression of the spirit, cannot be so simply determined. As an expressive function, it is always somewhat veiled, and as an instrumental function, it always includes the factor of indolence. Frankl makes an interesting comment in reference to this psychosomatic tendency, which he also disparages: "Only a 'glorified' body is representative of the spiritual person; the body of 'fallen' man, however, presents a shattered, and, therefore, distorted mirror."[5]

---

[5] Frankl, TT, 45.

Frankl believes that the wave of enthusiasm in psychosomatic medicine, might better be, at least partially, channeled in the direction of psychohygiene. Just as it is demonstrably true that some psychic states lower the immunity of the body to certain diseases, so it is conversely true, that certain other psychic states, such as joy, raise the immunity, and this evidence should be utilized, especially in educational and social areas.

D. *Organ Neurosis*

Organ neuroses are illnesses in which the symptomatology is physical, while the causal factor is psychic. This may be included in Frankl's definition of neurosis, in the "narrow" sense: *Neurosis is a psychogenic illness.*

In situations, such as heart palpitation, or any other physical symptom with no attendant pathology, the causal factor may be a psychological process. These are traditionally known as cases of hysteric conversion. Since the underlying pathology is the same as that of the more common neuroses, it will be discussed in the next section.

At this point, it may be well to remark that Frankl obviously accepts a theory of psychophysical interactionism in some phases of his writing, such as in the discussion of neuroses and their effect upon the body. On the other hand, in other areas of logotherapeutic teaching (as we have already pointed out), such as anthropology, especially where he sets the spiritual dimension over against the psychophysicum, he seems to repudiate interactionism in favor of a parallelism. He is not unaware of this, however, and feels that, in a heuristic system, these apparently contradictory theses are appropriate in their respective cases. From a scientific point of view, he feels that, just as light in modern physics must be considered both a "wave" and a "bundle," the evidence must be set forth only as systematically as its limits will allow. He would, perhaps, in this respect, think Emerson's famous phrase concerning "foolish consistency, the hobgoblin of little minds," quite apt.

E. *Neurosis*

Neurosis, which is the primary area of the application of Logotherapy as a treatment method, is that state of illness in which both the symptoms and the etiological factors are psychological, or originate in the psychic dimension of human personality. Frankl indicates that the term "neurosis" has had a wide and varied usage, and thus has, in some circles, been brought into disrepute as a scientific term. However, it has proven to be ineradicable, and in Logotherapy it is used in both a broad and narrow sense. The narrow sense is referred to in the above definition, and will be considered in this section, while the broader concept of neurosis will be discussed in a later section.

Neuroses are not, contrary to popular, and occasionally professional, opinion, caused by psychological complexes, conflicts, or traumatic experiences. Psychological "pressure" in itself is not a causal factor, although it may well precipitate a neurotic illness. "That complexes, conflicts, and trauma are pathogenic can simply not be the case because they are ubiquitous. What is commonly held to be pathogenic is in reality pathognomic; rather than causes of sickness, they are more its signs."[6] As a matter of fact, a relief from pressure is more often liable to provide the conditions for the outbreak of a neurosis than does even very difficult pressure. Frankl

---

[6] Frankl, HB, 720.

cites many examples throughout his books of personal breakdowns precipitated by release from pressure. Many persons,
for example, who were able to bear up under the critical
strain of concentration camp experiences, with their inde-
scribable threats to personal welfare, and existence itself,
suffered neurotic or psychotic breakdowns immediately following release.

It may well be for some people that an increase of pressure
has a prophylactic effect, just as an old architectural structure may often be stabilized by an increase of weight upon it.

Thus the commonly supposed causes of neuroses are usually
merely revelations of neurotic experience. Frankl uses the
analogy of a reef which is revealed with the ebbing of the
tide. Its appearance is obviously not the cause of the tide
going out, but rather, its effect. In neuroses the underlying
cause is more closely related to a developmental defect in
the personality structure.

Anxiety is an inevitable neurotic component. For Kierkegaard this anxiety was the "dizziness of freedom." Rollo May,
who has written an interesting and informative book on the
subject, indicates that "anxiety is the experience of the threat
of imminent non-being."[7] Frankl sees this experience of
anxiety as a factor which both originates and sustains the
neurotic chain of events.

In the neurotic there is also the tendency to absolutize
relative values in his daily life.[8] His failures are often spun
into strong cords, far beyond their due proportion of importance, and woven into a curtain of despair, which separates him from his goals and aspirations. In Existential An-

---

[7] May, et al, *Existence,* A New Dimension in Psychiatry and Psychology, 1958, Basic Books, New York, p. 50.

[8] This aspect of etiology has been emphasized by I. A. Caruso:
Psychoanalyse und Synthese der Existenz, Herder, Vienna, 1952.

alysis, however, there is hope, for man is seen as a *"facultative"* being and not a mere *"fact."* As a facultative being, he may be defined as one who can always become other than his present state (*Immer-auch-anders-werden-konnen*).[9]

The neurotic individual misunderstands himself, however, and fatalistically assumes that he is what he is and cannot change. He does not realize his existence as a human being. "To exist is to go beyond one's self, to transcend one's self, whereby the person steps out of the plane of the somatopsychic and, through the sphere of the spiritual, comes to himself."[10]

F. *Typical Neurotic Patterns*

According to Logotherapy, neurotic illnesses are initiated as a reaction to a physical state, or a psychological experience. There can be observed in neurotic behavior, a typical reaction pattern whose common denominator is anticipatory anxiety (*Erwartungsangst*). This is not seldom the real pathogenic factor in neurotic etiology. "The impact of functional illnesses, as well as the banal organic diseases, upon the psychological can easily be explained by the entrance of anticipatory anxiety. As soon as this fatal 'mechanism' begins to operate, every disease, and not only functional illnesses, can become 'secondarily neuroticized.' "[11]

A fleeting, and often harmless symptom may become the central focus of the patient's attention, and the neurotic cycle begins. Any momentary failure in function may also serve as the focussing point. The symptom is followed by the fear that the symptom will reoccur. This fear, in turn, rein-

---

[9] Frankl, TT, 169.
[10] Frankl, HB, 665.
[11] Frankl, UM, 9.

forces the symptom, which also strengthens the fear. "In the devil's circle which has closed, the patient himself is enclosed; he weaves himself in, as in a cocoon."[12]

A concrete case cited from Frankl's records will clarify this process: A young physician, suffering from a severe hidrophobia (fear of perspiring), came to us for treatment. He had been for a long time somewhat *vegetativ labil*. One day he extended his hand in greeting his chief of staff, and then noticed that he was perspiring profusely. The next time that he was in an analogous situation, he expected an outbreak of sweat, and this anxious expectation forced the sweat into the pores, whereby the vicious cycle was closed: the hyper-hidrosis provoked the hidrophobia, and the hidrophobia fixated the hyper-hidrosis.[13]

Frankl indicates three important neurotic patterns: Anxiety neuroses, obsessive-compulsive neuroses, and sexual neuroses. Other types of neurotic reactions are encountered in practice, but these are the dominantly typical ones.

1. Anxiety Neurosis Reaction Pattern

The well known statement of Roosevelt, that "the only thing we have to fear is fear itself," is very pertinent to anxiety neuroses. Patients themselves often mention an anxiety about being anxious. They have an anxious expectation that an anxiety attack, which they have already had, will reoccur. The initial anxiety has its somatic cause, but no psychological reason. The secondary anxiety, the anticipatory anxiety, on the other hand, has no "cause," in the sense of an immediate stimulating event, but it soon develops a rationale, or at least a rationalized ground, as the patient

---

[12] Frankl, TT, 59.
[13] Cf. Frankl, TT, 60.

thinks some reasons for it. And if he should not have such reasons, in other words, if his fears are primarily objectless, he soon will seek — and find — a reason.[14]

It is typical of anxiety, the objectless, or "groundless" threat of personal danger, or destruction, to seek a ground. When this occurs, the object "chosen" becomes known as a phobia. In Logotherapy, there are three general phobic tendencies which are dealt with in particular; these are not exclusive, nor exhaustive, categories of the reduction of anxiety, but rather, those which are most commonly observed in psychotherapeutic practice. They often specifically underlie agoraphobic cases: the fear of collapsing (*Kollapsphobie*), or the fear of being in an open place; the fear of a heart attack (*Infarktphobie*); and the fear of having a cerebral shock, or a "stroke" (*Insultphobie*).

All of these phobic groups, it may be observed, which serve as the ground for anxiety neuroses, refer to death, or physical damage, which would subsequently lead to death. It is sometimes amusing to note the particular phobic objects, and how they may be substituted. Frankl cites such a case: "A pre-climacteric patient was treated by us concerning an astraphobia — she was afraid of lightning. Upon being asked what she feared in winter, when there was no lightning, she replied, 'Then I don't suffer from lightning, but, instead, am afraid of cancer.' "[15]

Some investigators postulate an underlying neuropathy, or psychopathy, as the basis for a predisposition to an anxiety neurosis. Frankl believes that this may be true, and, as a

---

[14] Frankl illustrates the difference between cause and reason by indicating that an onion is no reason for crying, but it may well be the cause of tear secretion. In addition, tickling is no reason for laughing (as a joke, or a ludicrous situation is), but it can very easily stimulate the laugh reflex.

[15] Frankl, TT, 65.

matter of fact, believes that he has discovered a close connection between hyperthyroid conditions and agoraphobia,
as well as between claustrophobia and a calcium deficiency.
However he insists that, even if this be granted, it is not to
be understood as a fatalistic situation, but rather, merely
the fact that some people, through inheritance or glandular
disturbance, are more prone to be victims of neurosis than
others. A psychohygienic environment can prevent such a
neurosis from originating, and the spiritual dimension of man
can be called upon to overcome it when it does occur.

Frankl posits anticipatory anxiety as the basic factor in
the etiology of the anxiety neuroses. This secondary reaction
to an original anxiety experience (*Angst vor der Angst*)
stimulates the victim to attempt to flee from this anxiety,
which, ironically, strengthens the vicious cycle in which he
is enmeshed, for flight causes the symptoms of the primary
anxiety to arise. Thus the more one struggles to escape the
symptoms, the more firmly, like the Chinese manacles which
become tighter with every effort to be free, do they ensnare
him.

2. Obsessive-Compulsive Reaction Pattern

This type of neurotic adjustment involves the patient in
either the inability to control his thought process, in which
he, for instance, cannot stop thinking a certain idea; an
unceasing impulse to perform some act, such as breaking a
store window; or an uncontrollable act, commonly observed in
repetitious washing of the hands, or rechecking of the gas
jets on the kitchen stove.

Whereas in the anxiety neurosis the prime factor is anxiety
of, or before, anxiety, which eventuates in an attempted
flight from the anxiety situation, and, hence, reinforces the

neurotic symptoms, the compulsive neurotic has anxiety concerning his compulsions, and attempts to fight against their inexorable demands. An analogous result occurs, however, for his struggle against the compulsions reinforce them, making them even more compelling.

Frankl believes that there is an underlying neuropathic factor in anxiety neuroses, and a psychopathic one in compulsive neuroses, the latter component is called an "anankastic" character. While these inherited factors can never be eradicated, they can be controlled. There is no necessity of neurosis among such persons.

The compulsive neurotic also is prone to select phobic objects unconsciously, in order to drain off the crippling anxiety. This anxiety is anxiety concerning one's self (*Angst vor sich selbst*) rather than the anxiety concerning anxiety (*Angst vor der Angst*) of the anxiety neurosis, but it is the same pathological anticipatory anxiety. Here the patient fears that his condition will lead to insanity, or that it is already a psychotic indication, and, therefore, is called psychotophobia. On the other hand, he may develop the phobic fear that he will commit a crime (*Kriminophobie*) against himself, by a suicidal act (*Suizidphobie*), or against someone else (*Homizidphobie*), which is, for example, often observed in the neurotic mother's fear that she may throw her child out of the window.

3. Sexual Neurotic Reaction Pattern

In contemporary society in which sexual potency, the dominant theme of literature, television, and other media of communication, plays such a significant role as a symbol of social status, one encounters many instances of neurotic disturbance of the sexual function. The neurotic male is unable to demonstrate his potency, and the female is unable to overcome her frigidity. Impotence, which is usually initially caused by some momentary physical condition, or perhaps a moral conflict, subsequently precipitates the anxiety that it will reoccur. The anticipated pleasure, which should be merely the effect of conjugal love, when elevated to the goal of action, eventuates in frustration. In the sexual neurotic, the *circulus vitiosus* brings about the symptom which the person is struggling to overcome. His fear of impotence, and the intense effort to attain potency, bring about the very impotence he fears.

In addition to the anticipatory anxiety of the sexual neurosis, which is common to all of the reactive neuroses, the neurotic condition is further reinforced by the tendency to a hyper-reflection of the act. This self-consciousness of the sexual process heaps further insurmountable obstacles in the way of successful completion of the act. This reminds one of the anecdote of the centipede who ran very well until he decided one day to observe just how he ran. The more he became conscious of the process, the more difficult it was to function, and finally he could only lie in the ditch in despair.

The three common reactive neuroses have a common factor of anticipatory anxiety in reference to certain more or less accidental experiences, and a subsequent struggle against, or flight from this primary anxiety situation. Frankl denotes the anxiety neurotic's flight from the symptoms as "wrong passivity," and the fight against the symptoms of compulsive neuroses, or the struggle for orgasm and potency in sexual neuroses, as "wrong activity." They are "wrong" because they bring about the very effect that they intend to avoid, and thus fortify the symptoms that they want to weaken. "Just as the wish is the proverbial father of the thought, so here the fear is the mother of the event."[16] This psychological fact soon causes the neurotic person to tumble into a spiraling descent into despair which cripples him for normal responsible living.

G. Iatrogenic Neurosis

There is a sub-group of the reactive neuroses which, in Logotherapy, are emphasized because they have a common precipitating factor. This factor is the *iatros*, the physician, himself.

The psychotherapist must ever be wary of inadvertently increasing the anxiety of his patients by inept treatment or unthinking suggestions. A recent patient in Frankl's clinic, for instance, mentioned that a previous analytic therapist had told her that she *apparently* would not carry out her obsessive-compulsion to harm her husband. In addition, she was informed that this was an aggressive reaction which should be abreacted. Therefore, she was directed to cut off a doll's head during one of the therapeutic sessions in order to alleviate this "death instinct." Both the assurance that she *probably* would not carry out her impulse, and the guidance toward working out this "instinct," greatly increased her anxiety. The *possibility* of really harming a husband is an extremely traumatic piece of advice for an obsessive-compulsive person, who makes a fetish of 100% certainty. In this case the patient might well have been informed that there was no possibility that she would carry out the impulse against which she was so desperately struggling.

Among the particular dangers of which the doctor must be aware are the use of mysterious technical jargon, secretive attitudes concerning the physical examination and diagnosis

---

[16] Frankl, TT, 60.

of the problem, and any other comments which may tend to increase the anticipatory anxiety of the patient, or his tendency to a hyper-reflection of the symptoms.

H. *Neuroses in a Broader Concept*

Frankl not only uses the term "neurosis" to include the psychogenic reactive neuroses, but also in a wider sense to cover a neurotic existence which may have its primary roots in other than the psychic dimension.

1. PSEUDO-NEUROSES

Frankl asserts that in his clinical practice he has discovered certain pathological problems which, though symptomatically appearing to be neurotic adjustments, are really based upon physical factors. This group is an exception to the outlined table of illnesses, since it has a physical etiology and a psychic symptomatology. Technically, therefore, they should be classified with the psychoses, but this cannot be the case for they do not exhibit a psychotic symptomatology. They are called, in Logotherapy, functional illnesses, or "pseudo-neuroses." Although these are also often "cryptosomatogenic," Frankl bases the diagnosis of a physical etiology with respect to the fact that these monosymptomatic problems usually reveal certain objective physical correlates, as well as often responding to specific medication.

They are the result of vegetative and endocrinal functional disturbances which are masked behind the apparently neurotic clinical picture. For the most part such cases are also overlaid with true neurotic problems, though they are primarily somatogenic. In Logotherapy, three groups of such pseudo-neuroses are presented.

a. Basedowoid Pseudo-Neurosis

This illness, which is the result of a hyperthyroid condition, is revealed symptomatologically as agoraphobia. In addition, the basic metabolism usually shows a significant increase.

The following is a case report from Frankl's clinic: "The patient suffered for five years with an oppressive agoraphobia. For six months she had been in psychoanalytic treatment by a lay analyst, and, finally, discontinued treatment due to the absence of any therapeutic improvement. On the contrary, her depression had deepened. Objectively the patient manifested a tremor of the fingers and fluttering of the eyelids. The thyroid area was enlarged and the basic metabolism was +44%. The patient received Dihydroergotamine-methansulfonate parenterally, and already on the next day, the injection had 'worked a miracle.' 'It had never occurred to me,' she said, 'that I would come so far so quickly.' After a few more injections she remained free from anxiety and remarked, among other things, that the terrible dreams, from which she had suffered earlier, had now disappeared. 'The psychoanalyst had, to be sure, interpreted the dreams,' she said, 'but they still remained terrible!' "[17]

b. Addisonoid Pseudo-Neurosis

This type of pseudo-neurosis is caused by a hypadreno-cortical condition. The psychic symptom is the feeling of depersonalization, with a psychadynamic syndrome, and usually accompanied by low blood pressure.

One of Frankl's patients described his symptoms as follows: "Nothing seems to be really taking place. I don't have the

---

[17] Frankl, TT, 49.

92 LOGOTHERAPY AND THE CHRISTIAN FAITH

feeling of 'being here.' It seems as if a wire inside of me has broken. Everything seems like a dream. My consciousness is too narrow. Self-consciousness is completely gone. I can't seem to find a real ego. I ask myself the question, Why am I 'I', and not someone else? Everything seems to be different and I seem strange to myself. My voice sounds so strange, and I feel as if my arms and legs didn't belong to me anymore. It is as if I stood apart from my body, or else didn't even have a body at all, rather more if I were just a spirit." This patient's blood pressure was very low. After a few days in which he received daily medication of desoxycorticosterone-acetate (DOC), he felt "wonderful": "Everything is normal, everything is again so near, so bright, so clear. My consciousness and thinking are sharpened, just like they used to be."[18]

In a similar case, a student declared, in reference to the therapeutic effect of DOC, "It cleared my brain, my thinking capacity is better."[19]

Another young patient, who for six years had been treated by a lay analyst (6 sessions per week) without improvement, was treated by Frankl. Medication with DOC brought about rapid improvement and the patient recovered from her depersonalization symptom, and, in addition, was very much improved physically (she was confined to bed at the beginning of treatment). She was soon able to continue her university studies, and finished a doctoral dissertation.[20]

c. Tetanoid Pseudo-Neurosis

This group of pseudo-neuroses is characterized by claustrophobia, "globus hystericus," and difficulty in breathing.

[18] Frankl, TT, 53.
[19] Frankl, TT, 53.
[20] Cf. Frankl, TT, 54.

Laboratory tests often reveal a positive Chvostek, and a potassium-calcium ratio greater than 2. In such cases Frankl reports successful termination of the problem with the administration of calcium and/or o-methoxyphenyl-glycerine-ether (Myoscain E).[21]

In some cases in which the clinical evidence indicates a possible pseudo-neurosis, but in which neither agoraphobia (basedewoid) nor claustrophobia (tetanoid) is manifested, Frankl sometimes bases a differential diagnosis on the ground of the following question: Which would be more terrifying to you, to stand alone out in an open square, or to sit in the center of a row of seats in a crowded theater? He reports successful use of the appropriate medication following this diagnostic inquiry.

Inasmuch as these pseudo-neuroses are often accompanied by a secondary neurotic reaction, psychotherapy is usually utilized simultaneously with the medication. This obviously makes unclear, in such cases, how much of any positive effect is to be attributed to the physical, and how much to the psychological therapy.

2. NOOGENIC NEUROSIS

In the spiritual dimension of man there often arises the condition of existential frustration, that is to say, a condition in which the will to meaning is frustrated. This may be due to a moral conflict, to a specific spiritual problem, or to an existential crisis in development, such as may be observed in adolescence and the climacteric experience. Inasmuch as persons who are suffering under such circumstances often

---

[21] Frankl developed this drug as the first tranquilizing medication to be used on the continent. Cf. "Zur Behandlung der Angst," *Wiener medizinische Wochenschrift*, 102, 535, 1952.

refer to the emptiness and pointlessness of life, this is also referred to, in Logotherapy, as existential vacuum.

This condition is not in itself pathological. As a matter of fact, Frankl believes that the spiritual dimension in itself is not subject to pathological problems. However, this vacuum may either cause neurotic conditions, or else provide the "space" in which they may abound. Such neuroses, in contrast to those of psychogenic origin, are called "noogenic neuroses." This term indicates their origin from the noetic, or spiritual, dimension of personality. "In cases of noogenic neurosis, we are dealing with psychological illnesses which are not, as the psychogenic neuroses, rooted in conflicts between different drives, or clashes of classic components such as the socalled id, ego, and superego. They are, rather, rooted in collisions between different values, or in the unrewarded longing and groping of man for that hierarchically highest value – an ultimate meaning of his life."[22]

Frankl believes that existential vacuum is particularly prevalent in modern times. The increase of automation has made it increasingly difficult for the average worker to view his production as a personal project, while the decrease of work hours, with its subsequent increase of leisure time, has further complicated the problem.

A typical instance of noogenic neurosis comes from Frankl's records: "The patient came to us on account of nervousness, crying spells, stuttering, excessive sweating, trembling, eyelid fluttering, and a loss of 16 pounds of weight in the previous four months. All this was grounded in a conflict of conscience between her marriage and her faith: which should she sacrifice to the other? She placed a high value upon a religious education for her children, while her husband, an

[22] Frankl, "Beyond Self-Actualization and Self-Expression," Journal of Existential Psychiatry, Vol. 1, No. 1, Spring 1960.

outspoken atheist, was set against it. In itself the conflict is human and not pathological, however, the effect of the conflict, the neurosis, is pathological."[23]

Existential frustration is a human condition. It is not an illness in itself, nor is it necessarily pathogenic. It becomes productive of illness only when there is an accompanying situation in the psychophysical organism, which "accommodates" the noogenic distress. The illness does not affect the spiritual dimension as such, but rather is manifest in this psychophysicum. "Noogenic neuroses are illnesses 'out of the spirit' (aus dem Geist), but they are not illnesses 'in the spirit' (im Geist)."[24] The frustration is existential and not pathological.

Frankl warns against a pathologism which does not distinguish what is human from what is diseased. Pressure and problems are universal human conditions and not, per se, abnormal. Actually they may engender good health and be antipathogenic. Existential vacuum, psychic conflict, or physical stress (Selye) are not the marks of disease, but rather the ubiquitous and perpetually recurring conditions of life. "Just as there is truth in spite of illness, so there is suffering in spite of health. Psychologism forgets the first factor, while what I call pathologism overlooks the second."[25]

The converse of pathologism, that every existential frustration is pathogenic, is denoted, in Logotherapy, as "noologism," and is also to be guarded against. The noologistic error is to presume that every neurosis has a spiritual cause. It is a spiritualism which finds every neurotic condition noogenic. "Next to the Scylla of psychologism lurks the Charybdis of noologism. While the psychologism projects the

23 Frankl, HB, 717.
24 Frankl, TT, 125.
25 Frankl, TT, 123.

spiritual from the unique human dimension to the plane of the merely psychic; the noologizer interprets the physical onesidedly and exclusively in the sense of an expression of the spiritual."[26]

Neuroses of the noogenic group are not the exclusive neurotic adjustments by any means. As a matter of fact, they are in a distinct, though significant, minority. In the Vienna polyclinic psychotherapeutic outpatient department the percentage of noogenic neuroses in the case load has averaged about 14%. Reports from two German university clinics are not far from this — Wurzburg Women's Clinic, 21%; Tubingen Neuro-Psychiatric Clinic, 12%.

These neuroses, stemming out of the spiritual dimension, have Logotherapy as the indicated treatment method. They reveal a vacuum which must be filled with objective meaning and values, in order to obviate the neurotic condition, and to safeguard the mental health of the individual.

3. THE COLLECTIVE NEUROSES

In an even broader sense than that of somatogenic pseudo-neuroses, or noogenic neuroses, Frankl also includes, in his systematic outline of neurotic illnesses, "collective neuroses." These are typical of modern man, and reveal certain symptomatic trends. While it is true that neuroses in the more narrow clinical sense (as well as psychoses) have not, contrary to public opinion, increased in the last few decades, there are in modern times, due to the extenuating social and political circumstances, "traits in the character of contemporary man, which may be termed neurosis-like, 'similar to neurosis.' "[27]

---

[26] Frankl, TT, 127.

[27] Frankl, "Collective Neuroses of the Present Day," *Internationales Journal für prophylaktische Medizin und Sozialhygiene,* June, 1958, Vol. 2, no. 3, p. 1.

These socalled collective neuroses manifest four major symptoms:

(a) An ephemeral attitude toward life. People tend to live from day to day, or from paycheck to paycheck, with no attempt at long range planning or organizing of their lives for the future. The uncertainty of life, which characterized the war era, has continued with the "peace" era. "People seem to be in the grip of a mid-century mood, the slogan of which is, 'apres moi la bombe atomique.' "[28]

(b) A fatalistic attitude toward life. While the first symptom assumes that it is not necessary to plan one's life, this attitude asserts that it is not even possible. Modern man seems to have finally accepted the class room theses of the last half century of positivistic materialism, which taught him that he was merely a product of his environment, or the necessary result of his instinctive drives. He is little cheered by the philosophic persuasions of Russell that, nonetheless, he should have "confident despair."

(c) Collectivist thinking. Modern man attempts to deny his personality, and submerge into society. He is willing to be a number rather than to bear the burden of responsibility that accompanies the bearing of a name. His loss of identity is not in order to be a more useful social atom, but rather, so that he can hide in the mass.

A community needs individual personalities, but the mass is entirely different; in the mass no personality is valued, or allowed to develop its uniqueness.[29] Collective institutions, such as world communism, thrive upon collectivist thinking, and suppress individual freedom, while reducing man, in the

---

[28] Ibid.
[29] Cf. Frankl, "Logotherapy and the Collective Neuroses," in: Progress in Psychotherapy, Vol. IV., edited by Massermann and Moreno, Grune and Stratton, New York, 1959.

name of brotherhood, to the level of the herd. Man, then, plods on like a robot, thinking only what he hears, saying only what he is told to say, and functioning with all the creative flair of a tooth on a gear wheel.

(d) Fanaticism. While the collectivist denies his own personality, the fanatic ignores the personality of others.[30] He wants no other opinion to prevail but his own. He wants his own personality to be the world order.

Frankl believes that these trends are world wide. "It may be that the problem of collective neuroses is more actual in Europe, but the danger, the danger of nihilism, is planetary and is in no way confined to one continent."[31] He says that the first two symptoms of the collective neuroses are more prevalent in the West, whereas the last two dominate the eastern world.

It is obvious that these "neuroses" do not enter into the clinical picture for treatment, but are indications rather for the fields of education and mental hygiene: However, inasmuch as the view of man as "authentic" in Logotherapy is counter to these trends, such a consideration as the collective neuroses is important in order to round out the theme of "Logotherapy and Mental Health." Logotherapy embodies the antidote for this "disease of our time," but its application must extend far beyond the borders of psychotherapy.

Logotherapy is primarily concerned, insofar as it is psychiatrically oriented, with the diagnosis and treatment of neuroses. Its anthropological presuppositions are kept clearly in mind during the diagnostic process. Though the primary constituting factor of the person, the spiritual dimension, is to be carefully considered in every situation of illness, it is not to be considered to the exclusion of the psychophysicum.

---

[30] Cf. Frankl, HP, 48 ff.
[31] Frankl, TT, 189-190.

"Neurosis is no noetic, no spiritual illness, no illness of man merely in his spirituality: much more is it always an illness of man in his unity and wholeness."[32] Actually the psychic dimension is the primary causal area of a true neurosis. However, every dimension of personality is always involved, in every experience, whether in normal or neurotic existence. The diagnosis is not to determine how much of each dimension is effective in any specific illness, but rather, in which dimension the primary cause lies. Only by this procedure, Frankl believes, can a purposeful treatment method be selected for careful application.

In summary, it may be stated that Frankl finds the etiology of neurosis in various aspects of the complex dimensional ontology of man. Careful examination and consideration can, however, produce a differential diagnosis which will greatly expedite the therapeutic process from sickness to health. However, unlike many existential approaches to mental illness, Logotherapy considers the diagnosis and phenomenological description merely the first step in existential analysis of the ailing human being. The next step, the healing process, shall now be set before us.

---

[32] Frankl, TT, 125.

CHAPTER V

LOGOTHERAPY AND HEALING

In Logotherapy, the emphasis upon the "whole man" is retained in the sphere of therapeutic activity. Though a single dimension may be isolated for a specific purpose, and considered a closed system momentarily, in, for example, the examination of neurological reflexes, or the performance of a surgical procedure, nevertheless, the therapist should, both before and after such special periods of narrowed attention, view the patient as a unique existential person, an individual with diverse dimensions.

Because of this personal approach, Frankl tries to avoid emphasis upon techniques in therapy. This emphasis has often reduced the therapeutic procedure to the level of a technician perfunctorily performing a task. The implied reduction of the patient to a mechanism is one of the most dangerous of pitfalls, from the perspective of existential therapy.

In addition, concentration upon methods often will lead the therapist into a dead end street in his practice. Success in any specific case may beguile him into supposing that through his method, he has finally discovered the royal road to mental health. However, the warm flush of victory may turn to cold chagrin, when the next patient, with similar symptoms, is not only not improved, but, perhaps, even adversely affected by an identical treatment method. That it is not really identical, and thus equally successful, is due to the fact of uniqueness of personality which circumscribes a host of variable and uncontrollable factors of which the therapist may be quite unaware.

Psychotherapy must, then, be viewed as an art, and not a clearly defined scientific procedure. The therapist must self-consciously endeavor to develop a sensitivity to the patient's emotional states, just as the musician is sensitive to tone, and the painter to color. The timeworn debate as to whether artistic talent can be taught and learned, or must be inherited, is certainly pertinent at this point. Frankl takes a mediating position: *psychotherapeuticus natus non est sed fit* (the "born" psychotherapist must nevertheless *become* one). "Psychotherapy, to be sure, involves an endowed talent, but this talent still needs proper training."[1]

Psychotherapists should always bear in mind the human character of the patient, and at the same time be armed with every available scientific technique, as well as an objective attitude in the therapeutic situation. The psychotherapeutic process is likened to a field of polar tension between "human closeness" and "scientific detachment," in which the therapist must avoid either extreme. "The therapist must neither let his will and power to help people lapse into mere sympathy, nor, conversely, repress his human interest in the other human being, whom society in general, and the patient in par-

---

[1] Frankl, LE, 80.

ticular, has entrusted to his care, by dealing with the patient merely in terms of technique."[2]

Frankl believes that within the limits of the unique individuality of the patient, and the personality of the therapist, psychotherapy can be both taught and learned.[3] The concepts of the various schools of psychotherapy should not be permitted to supercede the patient's uniqueness by fitting him into some Procrustean bed of psychotherapeutic dogma, and the psychotherapeutic student, meanwhile, must not forget that there are no "typical" cases to be treated in a "typical" fashion. In addition, it must be noted that though the attainment of a thorough knowledge of psychotherapeutic concepts is extremely important, it is not sufficient apart from a thorough clinical experience.

Frankl has adapted the psychotherapeutic interview to teaching purposes by conducting actual therapeutic sessions which are sent "live" via microphone and loudspeaker to the lecture hall, as well as through the use of tape-recordings. The patient is made aware of the unseen presence of his audience, and is assured that the transmitted voice tone changes will protect his anonymity before the students. The patient soon forgets the extraneous factor in the therapeutic atmosphere, and the would-be therapists are enabled to "observe" first hand the all important existential "socratic dialogue" of psychotherapy.

Another important factor, in addition to the patient, in the therapy setting is the therapist himself. The point of view which holds that the therapist can remain a neutral entity,

---

[2] Frankl, "Paradoxical Intention: A Logotherapeutic Technique," *American Journal of Psychotherapy*, Vol. XIV, No. 3, July 1960.

[3] Cf. Frankl, "Ueber Lehrbarkeit und Lernbarkeit des Psychotherapie," *Festschrift zum 70 Geburtstag von Prof. Dr. Otto Pötzl*, Innsbruck, 1949.

or at most a mere "reflector of the patient's emotional distress," is neither possible nor desirable. Whether he wishes or not, the personality of the therapist, as a conscious, or unconscious, expression of his attitudes, emotions, and even philosophy of life, will make an impact upon the patient. "Psychotherapy is an equation with two unknowns: psi = x + y, whereby one unknown is the unpredictable moment of the personality of the physician, and the other the individuality of the ill person."[4]

Frankl is not convinced that a long range training analysis is a requisite for a psychotherapeutic vocation, though he, of course, believes that any person who intends to be a psychotherapist should have his vocational motives, and his personality structure, thoroughly and frankly evaluated through interviews with his psychiatric tutors. He believes that the practice of expensive and time consuming training analyses will, in a few years, be looked upon as a bygone historical fad.

In view of these variables in the psychotherapeutic equation, no universally effective technique is possible. Some therapists do not have the ability to use certain techniques, and some techniques are unsuitable for certain patients. Therefore psychotherapy must, and should, remain primarily an existential relationship of counselor and counselee. Techniques are ever secondary and must not be allowed to obscure this relationship.

On the other hand, in spite of the plethora of ideas in support of contemporary phenomenological and existential psychotherapy, there is a remarkable dearth of practical procedures presented as therapeutic tools. One may look in vain in many of the presentations of "existential analytic" psycho-

---

[4] Frankl, LE, 80.

therapies for a hint of technique. Much is said about the uniqueness of "being-in-the-world" and the phenomenology of inauthentic, or pathological, existence, but little about specific treatment. "Those who read works on existential analysis as handbooks of technique are bound to be disappointed. They will not find specifically developed practical methods."[5] One would almost think that such authors become so fascinated by the mysteries of existence that they forget the task at hand.

Logotherapy, however, while carefully keeping the "whole man" in mind, is an explicit therapeutic theory. It seeks to carry out the psychotherapeutic vocation with goal directed methods, selected in the light of careful diagnosis. Thus, the particular treatment must be appropriate to the body, psyche, or spirit, depending upon the primary causal factors of the illness. Inasmuch as neuroses are often "mixed," with multiple causation, simultaneous therapy in different ontological dimensions is often in order.

A. General Considerations in Therapy

Logotherapy is from the outset a therapy which involves the spiritual nature of man. It calls upon this distinctly human ability to transcend oneself (cf. page 60) and, thus to put "distance" between the patient and his illness. "He" is not sick, but rather only "has" an illness. In neurotic states the patient experiences the feeling that the illness "has" him, and Logotherapy appeals to the spiritual power, the opposing power of the spirit (Trotzmacht des Geistes) to change the situation. "The requirement, in the field of medicine, to consider the spiritual in man can only be fulfilled by a psycho-

---

[5] May, Rollo, et al, Existence, A New Direction in Psychiatry and Psychology, Basic Books, Inc., 1958, p. 76.

therapy 'derived from the spiritual' (*vom Geistigen her*) which I have defined as Logotherapy, or a psychotherapy 'directed to the spiritual' (*auf Geistiges hin*), denoted as Existential Analysis."[6]

The neurotic patient is haunted by his symptoms, and the anxiety and fear incited by them, makes his life miserable. Logotherapy, though not a symptomatic treatment in the generally accepted (and generally disparaged) sense of the term, often takes these symptoms as a starting point. It seeks to change the attitude of the patient to his symptoms, and thus change the effect of the symptoms upon him. "Insofar as Logotherapy does not treat the symptom directly, but rather attempts to bring about a change of attitude, a personal reversal of attitude toward the symptom, it is a truly personalistic psychotherapy."[7]

Logotherapy is an appellative therapy. It appeals to the spiritual dimension in man. Therefore, it is in this sense somewhat more "directive" than most psychotherapeutic theories on the American scene. This is not to be understood, according to Frankl, as being more "direction giving," but, rather, as a more active role played by the therapist. An anecdote concerning logotherapeutic practice is told concerning the difference between Frankl's Existential Analysis and psychoanalysis: In psychoanalysis the patient lies on a couch and tells the analyst things which are disagreeable to say, while in Logotherapy the patient sits in a chair and is told things which are disagreeable to hear! This is, of course, a caricature of the actual situation, but it does give an indication of the more active role of the logotherapist in analysis. Perhaps this change of emphasis will serve to counterbalance to a degree the extremists that "outroger" Rogers himself,

---

[6] Frankl, UM, 2.
[7] Frankl, UM, 34.

and thus become almost non-participants to the therapeutic situation!

Insofar as Logotherapy has as its central therapeutic thesis the appeal to the spiritual in man, it is directed primarily toward neurotic disturbances. However, it may also serve as a supportive therapy in psychotic illnesses, to the extent that the person is not "hidden" behind the disoriented and/or bizarre psychotic symptoms. "Logotherapy with (*bei*) psychoses (there is really no Logotherapy *of* psychoses) is essentially a therapy directed to the aspect of personality which remains healthy, really a treatment of the attitude of the healthy factor in the ill person over against that which has become diseased; for the healthy remainder is not subject to sickness, and the aspect which diseased is, in the sense of psychotherapy (and not merely Logotherapy) not treatable (rather is open only to physical therapy)."[8]

That the person may, even in badly deteriorated cases, have a value achieving attitude which reveals this "psychonoetic antagonism" is indicated by an elderly schizophrenic patient who, when asked about the degree of difficulty of her hallucinatory auditory symptoms, replied that they were hard to bear, but it was, in any case, better than being deaf![9]

One of the more practical possibilities of Logotherapy is its short term analysis. The average number of therapeutic sessions per patient at Frankl's clinic is eight. This figure includes those patients (75.7% of the total case load over a two year period) who were cured, or improved to the degree that no further treatment was required. Contrary to the supposition that short term therapy is necessarily superficial therapy, Frankl has demonstrated the long range effective-

[8] Frankl, HB, 679.
[9] Frankl, TT, 171.

ness of logotherapeutic treatment through periodic follow up
reports of former patients.[10]

Certain general features characterize every psychotherapeutic practice. In Logotherapy,[11] five initial axioms of
treatment are detailed:

1. The patient must be permitted to talk out his problem.
This will give the patient opportunity for relief of emotional
pressure, and will provide for the therapist important data
as background for subsequent treatment.

2. A thorough physical examination should be carried out.

3. A negative report of this examination should not be
explained in such a way as to give *iatrogenic* strengthening
of the neurotic problem. Frankl believes that the saying,
"one of the most widespread diseases is the diagnosis," is not
too far afield. "The ill person can, under certain circumstances, for instance, in the word 'cardioneurosis,' see a hypo-
chondriacal bogeyman, just as well as in 'angina pectoris.' "[12]

4. Conversely, a negative report which is shrouded with
mystery and silence can also affect the person adversely. All
too often the patient's imagination construes silence as the
withholding of dreadful news, and thus his condition is
worsened.

5. The therapist should also avoid referring to the patient's
condition as "only a neurosis," "just nerves," or, worse to
say, "only in the patient's mind." Though subjective, the
symptoms are nevertheless real and, when summarily waved
aside by some such phrase, will only bring a protest reaction
from the patient. This will, in turn, make therapy much
more difficult. Frankl suggests some such approach as follows to report the negative finding of the physical examina-

10 Cf. Frankl, MS, 39 ff.
11 Cf. Frankl, PP, 22 ff.
12 Frankl, PP, 23.

tion: "Fortunately there is no organic disease indicated. This means that your suffering, though unpleasant, is not dangerous."

The therapist should always be an accepting and optimistic person. Frankl believes that one should be as positive as possible with the patient in order to utilize the "power of positive thinking" in the therapeutic situation. For instance, in the realm of physical functioning, it can be demonstrated that a patient with a slightly high blood pressure will often register a reduction if he is told that his blood pressure is "about normal," whereas, if he is told that it is high, it will go still higher.[13]

The therapist should never moralize, nor agree with self reproaching attitudes of the patient. He should deal with the patient as though he were what he should be, rather than what he is. Goethe spoke wisely: When we regard people as they are, we make them worse; but when we regard them as they should be, we make them what they can be.

B. *Physical Therapy*

Logotherapy, in its psychiatric clinical sphere of activity, includes chemotherapy as a basic tool. Frankl himself was the first in the continental European area to develop a tranquilizing medication in psychiatric practice.[14]

Moreover, specific medication is indicated in the cases of pseudoneuroses, as we have already mentioned in the last chapter, with respect to their primary somatogenic etiology.

Inasmuch as the pseudo-neuroses are often "overlaid" with secondary neurotic factors, a simultaneous psychotherapy is

---

[13] Cf. Frankl, DE, 110.
[14] Cf. Frankl, "Zur Behandlung der Angst," *Wiener Medizinische Wochenschrift*, 102, 535, 1952.

applied. This "pincer movement" is reported to be both rapid and highly successful. It should be noted, however, that such a procedure obviates the possibility to evaluate the relative merits of either therapeutic approach. For this reason Frankl uses, in his clinic, as the author observed, the procedure of applying only one therapy at a time — either drug, or psychological — as long as either the structure of the case, or the range of therapy, has not been definitely determined.

Electric shock therapy is also often utilized in Frankl's logotherapeutic clinic, especially in cases where endogenous depression is apparent. Also, though Frankl is quite conservative in this respect, leucotomies, or pre-frontal lobotomies, are sometimes recommended as radical treatment methods. In regard to such "psychosurgery," he says, "In this connection, I should like to stress (or should I better say confess?) that, according to my convictions, there are occasional cases in which this operation is the only way to help. . . . In one case, to give a specific example, the patient was so handicapped by severe obsessive-compulsive symptoms that psychotherapy, and a subsequent series of electro-shock treatments had proved in vain. Since the operation, however, (more than ten years ago) she has been fully symptom free, with no signs of character change or other undesirable side effects accompanying the beneficial results."[15]

C. *Logotherapy as a Non-specific Therapy of Neuroses*

Logotherapy is considered a non-specific therapy in cases of psychogenic neurotic reactions. It directs itself neither to the symptoms themselves, nor to the historical trauma

---

[15] Frankl, "Paradoxical Intention: A Logotherapeutic Technique," *American Journal of Psychotherapy*, Vol. XIV, No. 3, July 1960.

which may have precipitated them, but rather, to the attitude of the patient toward his symptoms.

As we have noted in the previous chapter, the prime factor in neurotic conditions, according to logotherapeutic teaching, is anticipatory anxiety, which, as the feared reoccurrence of a previous anxiety producing experience, ironically causes the feared experience to come to pass. This secondary anxiety, in anxiety and phobic neuroses, stimulates the person to flee from the object or situation identified with the primary anxiety of the original experience. Such flight, or as it is called in Logotherapy, "wrong passivity," closes a vicious circle in which the anxious expectation precipitates the feared experience, and the experience of the symptoms, in turn, reinforces the anticipatory anxiety. In obsessive-compulsive neuroses, this "mechanism" is similar except that the person, rather than fleeing, performs "wrong activity" by warring against his neurotic impulses.

In neuroses involving functional disturbances, such as sexual neurosis, this anticipatory anxiety, centered upon the possible non-functioning of the sexual, or in the cases of insomnia, of the sleep process, stimulates a *forced intention* which disrupts the normal function. In addition, there is usually a compulsive *self-observation*, an increased *attention* which compounds the inability. "We see an interesting parallel in which anticipatory anxiety *makes true* precisely what the patient fearfully had expected, while an excess of self-observation of one's own functions, as well as an exceeding amount of intention to the fulfillment of these functions, *makes impossible* the execution of them."[16] That these become obstacles to functional fulfillment is due to the fact

---

[16] Cited from a lecture by Frankl on *Paradoxical Intention*, given at the University of Vienna, Spring semester, 1960.

that increased attention or intention of autonomic functions is self defeating.

The two therapeutic methods of Logotherapy which are designed to break this neurotic "feedback" mechanism which is sustained by the anticipatory anxiety are known as "paradoxical intention" and "de-reflection."[17]

1. PARADOXICAL INTENTION

Paradoxical intention is based directly upon the anthropological principles of Logotherapy. It is grounded in the human ability to exist, to transcend the plane of the psychophysicum through what Frankl calls psychonoetic antagonism, or what is also often called "the defiant power of the spirit." Thus paradoxical intention is a true therapy "of the spirit." Hereby the patient objectifies and ironizes his anxieties. This breaks the vicious cycle, and thus causes the neurotic symptoms to disappear. The radical change of attitude toward the symptoms, from anxiety to irony, causes a radical change in the personal functioning of the patient.

The patient is encouraged to intend, or wish for, precisely that of which he is afraid. Even if this takes place for only a few seconds, it takes the "wind out of the sails" of the neurotic anxiety. Two case reports from Frankl's clinic will demonstrate the method and merit of paradoxical intention in phobic and obsessive-compulsive cases, respectively:

"A young physician suffered from a severe hidrophobia. One day as he reached out to shake hands with his hospital superior, he noticed that he was perspiring to a conspicuous degree. The next time, in an analogous situation, he expected the outbreak of perspiration, and the anticipatory anxiety

---

[17] The logotherapeutic school utilizes other standard psychotherapeutic methods as well, though these two are distinctively related to an existential view of man.

forced the 'nervous sweat' through the pores. Our hidro-
phobic patient was instructed by us, in case of the occurrence of the anticipatory anxiety, to resolve immediately to
really sweat! 'The last time I perspired less than a liter,' he
said to himself at the time (as he later reported), 'but now
I'll sweat out ten liters!' And the result? After suffering for
4 years with his phobia, he was cured fully and finally (after
only one appointment) in less than a week."[18]

The following is a tape-recorded report of a patient:
". . . Once I had forgotten to lock the door and when I re-
turned home it was open. That frightened me very much.
After that, whenever I left the house, I couldn't get rid of
the feeling that the door was still open. I would go back
again and again to check it. So it went on for twenty years.
I knew that the obsession was silly, for every time I went
back the door would be locked, but I couldn't seem to keep
from obeying the impulse. Life became unbearable! Since
I had that (!) interview with Dr. Becker, however, things
have changed completely. Whenever I have the compulsion
to check whether or not the door is locked, I say to myself,
'What if the door *is* open! Let them steal everything in the
whole apartment!' and at that moment I am able to ignore
the impulse and go calmly on my way."[19]

Paradoxical intention is not a persuasion method in the
traditional sense of the term at all, in spite of the fact that
it has been so (mis-)understood. One misses the point in
such a criticism, for in many respects paradoxical intention
is the exact opposite of therapeutic persuasion. Whereas
persuasive techniques would try to convince the patient that

---

[18] Frankl, TT, 85. The same case has been cited on page 10,
chap. 4, with reference to the significance of anticipatory anxiety in
its etiology.

[19] Cf. Frankl, MS, 38-39.

"it can't happen to me"; paradoxical intention instructs the patient to wish, paradoxically, that "it shall happen to me."

The role of humor in this logotherapeutic technique is very important. Nothing is so effective in putting distance between a person and his problems as a humorous experience. The patient almost invariably laughs when he first hears, and first attempts to carry out, the instructions of paradoxical intention. The therapist should utilize this situation as much as possible, for it is an important medium of psychonoetic antagonism. When the patient is able to laugh at his anxieties, he is on the road to improvement. "The physician should not be embarrassed to dictate to the patient, nor even to demonstrate, what the patient should say to himself. When the patient smiles, we say to him, 'When you say all this to yourself, you will laugh, and will have won the battle.'"[20] Frankl believes that humor is a unique existential capacity of man, and an excellent mode of self detachment.

In neuroses involving functional disturbances, paradoxical intention may also be applied. After a general explanation of the trustworthiness of the organism, i.e., that it can be depended upon, for instance, to get enough sleep automatically, the patient may be instructed to try to stay awake, to intend not to perform sexually,[21] or to attempt to stutter. In this manner the anticipatory anxiety is thwarted, and the organism, relieved of the neurotic pressure, is enabled to function normally.

The following will illustrate the use of paradoxical intention in a case of the functional disturbance of speech:

---

[20] Frankl, TT, 87.
[21] Frankl does not himself use paradoxical intention in cases of sexual neurosis, although, at least theoretically, it should be equally helpful.

"Horst S. is seventeen years of age. His stuttering problem began four years previously during a class recitation. His schoolmates laughed at him and this became a very traumatic experience. Subsequently his speech difficulty occurred with increasing frequency. Finally he refused to attempt oral recitation altogether. One year ago he was treated by a nerve specialist by means of 'autogenous training' (relaxation exercises after J. H. Schultz of Berlin). There were no beneficial results, however, and the case was referred to Dr. Manfred Eisenmann of Freiburg in Breisgau. He explained to the patient the basic mechanism of anticipatory anxiety as involved in the pathogenesis of the trouble, as well as the false attitude adopted toward it. Though the patient was very pessimistic, Dr. Eisenmann succeeded in getting him to say to himself, whenever the stuttering anxiety gripped him, 'Oh! I'm afraid that I'll stutter on a 'b' or a 'p'!; well, today I think I'll stutter through the whole alphabet for a change!' At first Horst merely laughed at the instructions, but later discovered that his laughter was the heart of the matter. When he could ironize his fears and thus put himself at a distance from them, he was actually detaching himself from his painful problem. He could not bring himself actually to try paradoxical intention until after the fifth interview. He finally succeeded, however, and, after only two more psychotherapeutic sessions, was able to continue classroom recitation free of any speech difficulty."[22]

Sometimes Frankl uses for short term therapeutic purposes, a combination of paradoxical intention and tranquilizing treatment. As an instance of such simultaneously somatopsychic procedures or, as he sometimes calls it, a therapeutic

[22] Cited from a lecture by Frankl on *Paradoxical Intention,* given at the University of Vienna, Spring semester 1960.

"pincer movement" attacking anticipatory anxiety as the main pathogenic factor, the following case is a good example:

"The patient, Josef M., bookkeeper, 41 years old, was treated for many months by several doctors and in several clinics without any therapeutic success; and now came to us in extreme despair and admitted that he was near to suicide. For years he suffered from a 'writers cramp' which had recently become so severe that he was in danger of losing his job. It seemed that only an immediate short term therapy could possibly alleviate the situation. The patient was assigned to the first assistant of the clinic, who recommended to him that he try to do just the opposite of what he usually did; namely, instead of trying to write as neatly and legibly as possible, to write with the worst possible scrawl. His theme was to be: 'Now I'll really show them how to scribble!' Simultaneously the patient took two tablets of Myoscain E (cf. page 93 above) three times daily. In less than 48 hours the patient was freed from his anticipatory anxiety (and still remains so after several months) as well as having completely overcome his 'writers' cramp.' 'I have tried to scrawl, but simply couldn't do it.' he reported. 'Now I can write freely again, I can continue working and supporting my family; — I'm so happy that I can hardly express myself.' "[23]

Paradoxical intention is an existential psychotherapeutic technique which utilizes the facultative power of human personality to "defy" the psychic or physical factors involved in the neuroses. This procedure dissolves the anticipatory anxiety, which so often is the prime factor, according to Logotherapy, in neurotic maladjustment. It can be applied in any situation where this type of anxiety is significant.

---

[23] Frankl, "Tranquilizer und Ataraktika bei neurotischen Stoerungen," *Die Aerztliche Fortbildung*, Vol. 10, No. 10, p. 4.

2. DE-REFLECTION

Whereas paradoxical intention is designed to counteract anticipatory anxiety, de-reflection is employed to neutralize the compulsive self-observation, or hyper-reflection, which is commonly an additional factor in neurotic reactions involving functional disturbances.

The primary aim is to divert the patient's attention from himself to the task at hand, or the partner involved. Contrary to the thesis entertained by some existentialist thinkers, that intensive self-reflection is the essence of existence, Frankl is convinced that it is really a phase of the neurotic process. Existing does not entail intensive, crippling self-consciousness, but rather, self-transcending decisions in reference to the objective world, and the persons and objects in it.

In paradoxical intention the patient *ironizes* his symptoms, while he learns to *ignore* them through de-reflection. The term itself has a negative connotation, though the technique is not primarily the turning *away* from the symptoms, but rather, the turning *to* positive activity. The patient is to be convinced of the trustworthiness of his psychophysical organism, or, as it may be stated in existential discourse, in him must be restored a basic trust in Being (*Urvertrauen zum Dasein*).[24]

The following two accounts will show this technique in a clinical setting:

a. Neurotic swallowing problem: "Miss B. compulsively observed the act of swallowing; having become uncertain, she anxiously expected that the food would 'go down the wrong way,' or that she would choke. Anticipatory anxiety and compulsive self-observation disturbed her eating to the extent that she became very thin. She was taught to trust her organism

---

[24] Cf. Frankl, MS, 41.

and its automatically regulated functioning. The patient was therapeutically de-reflected by the formula, 'I don't need to watch my swallowing, because I don't really need to swallow, for actually I don't swallow, but rather *it* does.' And thus to the *it*, the unconscious, she was able to leave the unconscious and unintentional act of swallowing."[25]

b. Neurotic speech disturbance: "Gerhardt B. is nineteen years old, and suffered since he was six with a speech disturbance which was occasioned during an electrical storm in which a bolt of lightning struck near him. From that instant until eight days later, he could not speak at all. He was treated psychoanalytically for five months, and had taken speech and breathing exercises for four additional months. We attempted to make one thing clear to him, and this was that he would have to give up the ambition to become a good orator. We further explained that to the degree in which he became resigned to being a poor speaker, he would, as a matter of fact, improve his speech. For then he would pay less attention to the 'how' and more to the 'what' of his speech."[26]

The positive goals of de-reflection are gained through an existential analysis of the patient. (A discussion of this process will take place in the next chapter.) Therefore, not only does the therapist divert the patient from attentiveness to his disturbance, but also to the meaningful goals in life which will fulfill his personality and his life task. Frankl believes that de-reflection involves not only a dissolution of compulsive self-observation, but also, a redirecting toward transcendent meaning and values.

The therapeutic benefit of such diversion is indicated in the statement by Allport that, "As the focus of striving shifts

25 Frankl, TT, 95-96.
26 Frankl, TT, 96.

from the conflict to selfless goals, the life as a whole becomes sounder, even though the neurosis may never completely disappear."[27] According to Frankl, however, that which does not completely disappear is not the neurosis, but rather the underlying character structure which is unchangeable (i.e., the anankastic component in obsessive-compulsive neurotic personalities). "The character structure itself is not a full fledged neurosis, for the full fledged neurosis is the result of the patient's inappropriate attitude toward those ideas which emerge out of the character structure."[28]

Existential analysis, as a psychotherapeutic approach, is a decided advance beyond psychoanalysis both practically and theoretically. "The way, which psychotherapy since Freud has come, is marked by two steps: the first step leads it from *automatism to existence,* the second from *autonomy to transcendence.*"[29] This recognition of the spiritual nature of man, in contrast to the theory that man's activity is the automatic expression of instinctive drives, may well be a revolutionary factor in modern mental health prophylaxis, and psychotherapy.

The two logotherapeutic techniques, paradoxical intention and de-reflection, are the means by which the two above-mentioned steps may be taken. Frankl considers these two methods as the effective therapeutic countermeasures to the "wrong passivity" and "wrong activity" of neurotic behavior. Paradoxical intention, the *ironizing* of symptoms, is made possible by means of "right passivity," while de-reflection, the

---

[27] Allport, Gordon, *The Individual and His Religion,* Macmillan, New York, 1956, p. 95.
[28] Cited from a lecture given at the University of Melbourne, Australia, in October 1957.
[29] Frankl, LE, 81.

ignoring of symptoms, is made possible through "right activity."

3. LOGOTHERAPY AND TRADITIONAL PSYCHOTHERAPY

There are two initial objections that may be brought against Logotherapy in regard to its therapy of psychogenic neuroses. The widespread influence of the psychodynamic interpretation of neurosis, and its companion, psychoanalytic treatment, brings Logotherapy into question as a therapy which is superficial because it neither gets at the roots of the neurotic problem, nor works long enough with the patient to secure for him a permanent cure. Gutheil indicates that objections such as these, though commonly held, are nonetheless based upon "the more common illusions of freudian orthodoxy, such as that the length of therapy is synonymous with the depth of therapy; that the depth of therapy depends on the frequency of interviews; that the results of therapy are proportionate to the length and depth of treatment; that the durability of results corresponds to the length of therapy."[30]

The need for an historical analysis is considered, in Logotherapy, a relatively rare occurrence.[31] The stress upon such an analysis is based upon a mistaken psychodynamic view of man, and the presumption that therapeutic success depends upon rooting out the past traumatic experiences that are related to a present neurotic problem. However, it is a common experience of the psychotherapist, that such unearthings, or the bringing of traumatic experiences, buried in the unconscious, to the surface, may have little or no therapeutic effect. There are those presently who question the

---

[30] Gutheil, *American Journal of Psychotherapy*, 1956, Vol. 10, pp. 552–6.

[31] Frankl concedes that it may be necessary, for instance, in cases of sexual perversion.

necessity of such an historical regression. "Although traditional psychotherapy has insisted that therapeutic practices
have to be based upon etiology, it is possible that certain factors might cause neuroses during early childhood and that
entirely different factors might relieve neuroses during adult-
hood."[32] Frankl goes beyond this and maintains that the
causal factor is not really the past experience, but rather it is
the presently effective anticipatory anxiety which is pathogenic. Thus there is no need for a long, time consuming
analysis. "When you can cut across the circle formation, you
need not concern yourself much with the underlying psychodynamic factors. They no longer have strength, for the main
pathogenic factor was the anticipatory anxiety, not the underlying psychic experience."[33]

Though these historical factors are related to the sub-
conscious motivation which underlies the symptom, one
might liken them to the roots of a plant which shrivel when
the stem is severed. Frankl believes that when the neurosis
is not symptomatically expressed, it will shrivel and die. As
opposed to the widespread warning as to the dire consequences of relieving symptoms without "digging down deep,"
one might well refer to the statement of J. H. Schultz —
"The frequently expressed misgiving, that cases of symptom
removal must necessarily be followed by substitute symptoms
or some other internal defection, is, in general, a completely
baseless assertion."[34] In this respect, however, it should be
again emphasized that Logotherapy is not directed toward the

---

[32] Weisskopf-Joelson, Edith, "Some Comments on a Viennese
School of Psychiatry," *Journal of Abnormal and Social Psychology*,
vol. 51, Nov. 1955, p. 702.
[33] Frankl; taken from a tape recorded conversation with Rev.
Kenneth Hildebrand, Central Church of Chicago, Summer, 1959.
[34] Schultz, *Acta Psychotherapeutica*, 1, 33, 1953.

removal of symptoms, per se, but rather, the change of attitude toward them. Thus the symptom removal is a side effect
of an existential decision.

The length of therapy is irrelevant in Logotherapy. In
practice the logotherapist discovers that relatively few sessions are needed. He does not deny that a long personality
analysis is both interesting and helpful, but feels that it is
not consistent with the pressing need for psychotherapy, and
the consequent demand upon the time of the busy therapist
(to say nothing of the great drain upon the purse of the
patient). Frankl would recommend rather, that the patient
come back to the therapist after a couple of weeks, or months,
or even years — whenever he needs new reassurance. At any
rate, the relationship between the therapist and patient (and
this means trust, and not dependence) endures after the
short term treatment has been terminated.

That short term therapy brings only temporary relief is
not empirically demonstrated. This excerpt of a tape-recorded
report of an obsessive-compulsive patient, who was treated by
paradoxical intention, will, rather, be opposing evidence:

". . . There was practically not one minute during the day
when I was free from the thought that I might shoot myself;
but after Dr. Frankl advised me to carry a loaded revolver,
even with the safety off, the whole situation changed. And
to think that I wouldn't even have dared so much as to look
at a loaded gun before! . . . I also was haunted by the idea
that I might break a store window. He told me to go right up
to the window with the intention of smashing it. When I did
this, the fear disappeared completely and I knew that I would
never go through with it. It all seems like a dream now; the
fears and impulses to do these things have all vanished"

(this report was given 20 years after the treatment, which consisted of a few sessions!).[35]

No doubt there will be some who will remain unconvinced that Logotherapy is "deep enough" or "long enough," but they will be forced to confess that Frankl is certainly not unaware of these criticisms, and also that he has amassed an imposing amount of theoretical and clinical evidence to support his break with the "traditions of the fathers."

D. Logotherapy as the Specific Therapy of Noogenic Neuroses

In noogenic neurosis, the patient has as a primary problem existential frustration, or existential vacuum. This condition is not in itself neurotic, but has, in these cases, caused neurotic symptoms, which are manifested through the psychophysical organism. Such neuroses are usually considered merely psychogenic by most therapists, who overlook their being rooted in the overwhelming feeling of meaninglessness in the life of the patient. The will to meaning, which sustains the spiritual dimension of personality, has been frustrated, and the therapeutic goal is to "fill" the accompanying "vacuum."

This, of course, involves Logotherapy in the realm of values. Inasmuch as psychotherapy historically has prided itself in its axiological, or value, neutrality, this is a very significant fact. Frankl is not at all apologetic, however, for he asserts that "a psychotherapy which claims to be free of values, is in reality merely blind to values."[36] He is, however, adamant in insisting that this does not involve Logotherapy

---

[35] Frankl, "Paradoxical Intention," *American Journal of Psychotherapy*, Vol. XIV, number 3, p. 529.

[36] Frankl, HB, 664.

in making value judgments for the patient. The logotherapist, rather, only broadens the value horizon of the patient,
in order that he may find values and life goals which will fill
up his hitherto empty existential condition.

A case report will make this clinical situation clearer:
" 'My husband is gone with the car, like he does every night.
I really feel sorry for him. He needs the excitement. Now
that he has it easier and is free at five o'clock, he is very
restless. We have a nice living room and a radio, but we
don't have anything to say to each other. Everything has
fallen through, everything is empty. Books aren't interesting,
and I fall asleep during the radio programs.' A few weeks
later, after treatment: 'I am well, completely well. I have
found myself and am out of danger. I am very happy. It
seems to me as if a great door had been opened to a dazzling
brightness. My heart is a blooming garden, into which I may
withdraw whenever I please. Now I am at peace. Everything
is all right. Life is glorious and wonderful.' "[37]

The patient is therapeutically de-reflected to objective
meaning and values, which obviate the existential frustration, and thus dry up the spring from which those noogenic
neuroses are flowing. Since the meaning and values, as such,
are revealed in existential analysis, we shall postpone a discussion of them until the next chapter.

In this chapter, we have observed that Logotherapy, contrary to many so-called existential psychotherapies, has an
explicit therapeutic procedure which is based upon its anthropological theory, and geared to its view of mental illness.
Though the human relationship of two persons, the therapist
and the patient, is the primary factor in the therapeutic
process, practical techniques and methods are requisite for

---

[37] Frankl, TT, 120.

efficient and goal directed treatment. Logotherapy, as a true psychotherapy "of the spirit," attempts to call upon the spiritual in man in order to re-establish most effectively good mental health and successful personal living.

Although therapy should be directed toward that ontological dimension of personality in which the primary causal factor lies, it is also true that the therapist is dealing with a single, individual person. Thus perfect health involves a harmony of the three basic dimensions of the human being. It sometimes occurs that the bringing of one dimension into balance, may cause another to recover spontaneously. This should be borne in mind in all therapeutic procedures and therapeutic goals.

Whereas the spiritual dimension, as the decisive, constitutive dimension of personality, plays such a primary role in man's existence, it is important to know to what extent his health is dependent upon the "balance" of this dimension. The therapist should know the significance of the transcendent moral impulse, revealed in the religious consciousness, the conscience, and also the extent of the spiritual resources available when one's destiny includes chronic ill health and/ or imminent non-being, or death. To this end, we turn to the "medical ministry" of Logotherapy .

CHAPTER VI

LOGOTHERAPY
AND THE MEDICAL MINISTRY

Logotherapy does not end with the resolution of neurotic problems. Its view of man as a spiritual being, with potentialities for abundant living, lead it far beyond the narrow scope of pathological problems. Frankl refers to this area of opportunity and responsibility, as the "medical ministry" (*Aerztliche Seelsorge*).

These possibilities of personality imply that the physician's role must extend beyond physical and psychological treatment in order to meet the needs of a meaningful and responsible life. "Therapy is concerned with something more fundamental (than cure), namely, helping the person experience his existence; and any cure of symptoms which will last must be a by-product of that."[1]

Existential frustration and existential vacuum, though not in themselves pathological, nor necessarily pathogenic, bring

---

[1] May, Rollo, et al, *Existence*, A New Direction in Psychiatry and Psychology, Basic Books, New York, 1958, p. 86.

existential crises which are very often today, in turn, brought to the physician. In addition, there are problems of incurable diseases, inoperable malignancies, and the imminence of death, which overflow the bounds of medical science, but which, nevertheless, confront medical men. Frankl believes that the physician can, and should, be prepared to bring relief to such people in distress. It is not an exclusive problem of the psychotherapist, but rather, a responsibility of everyone who deals with suffering patients.

There are no life situations which are not undergirded with potential meaning and value. The patient must be brought to a consciousness of the meaning options and then he will be able to "exist," then he will be able to fulfill his life task. As Nietzsche observed in his oft quoted aphorism: He who has a *why* to live, can endure almost any *how*.

To help a person find meaning for his life involves, of course, values and value judgments. This has been considered a forbidden area of activity for the psychotherapist, who often prizes his objectivity and neutrality to value systems. Frankl insists, however, (as we have already noted) that a "psychotherapy which considers itself to be free of values, is in reality merely blind to values."[2]

Rather than to avoid values, in Logotherapy, it is, on the contrary, deemed a pressing necessity to bring to the consciousness of the patient the meaning and values which will give him something for which to live, and the stimulus for an authentic existence.

The discussion of the medical ministry of Logotherapy will be presented in three phases. The existential analysis of basic human experiences will be followed by a consideration of the treatment of unavoidable suffering and despair.

---

[2] Frankl, TT, 148.

Finally, the role of the logotherapist in bringing unconscious religious values to the consciousness of the patient will be set forth.

A. Basic Human Experiences

Psychotherapy is generally conceived as the effort to bring unconscious psychic events to the surface of consciousness. Logotherapy, on the other hand, seeks to bring to awareness the unconscious spiritual factors of the patient's personality, while Existential Analysis is the endeavor to enable the patient to become conscious of his responsibility. "By definition Existential Analysis aims at 'being conscious of having responsibility (*Bewusst-sein des Verantwortung-habens*).'"[3] This responsibility is the main factor of human existence and is a central consideration of every important "stage along life's way."

The meaning of a person's life, his life task, must be discovered in conjunction with his responsibility as a human being. Thus the logotherapist is not content merely to deal with the clinical complaints and psychotherapeutic needs of the patient. "Beyond this it is a task of logotherapeutic endeavor to stimulate concrete meaning possibilities; this, however, requires an analysis of the concrete human existence (*Dasein*), the personal existence of the patient in question, in a word, an existential analysis."[4]

Not only is this analysis possible in reference to a particular person, but it may also be applied to mankind; such an analysis would, of course, amount to an essentialism rather than existentialism. "Existential Analysis means not only the explication of ontic existence, but rather also an ontological

---

[3] Frankl, LE, 39.
[4] Frankl, MS, 53.

explication of what existence is."[5] This should not be taken to mean that there is an "average man," or a man in general, but only that each human existence, though unique, must encounter certain universal phases of existence. The responsibility entailed in these phases gives them rich and meaningful potentialities for personal development.

1. THE MEANING OF LIFE

Only a human being can question the meaning of life.[6] Insects and animals cooperate in symbiotic relationships, and carry out intricate instinctive activities, but never pose philosophical questions. Though lemmings rush headlong into the sea, and certain death, it is never because of despair concerning the vicissitudes of life.

It is neither abnormal nor morbid to ask such a question, for, given the ability to transcend oneself in existential reflection, it is a perfectly obvious inquiry. There are those who seem too busy living to question life, but most people at one time or another pause from the turmoil of the day, and ask themselves. What does it all mean anyway? Not everybody can find a satisfying answer, however, and some cannot contentedly return to a task that may well be much ado about nothing.

On the other hand, there are many persons who try to avoid asking about the meaning of life. They usually try to evade the inquiry by either denying that the question has meaning, or by ignoring it altogether. The positivistic denial of the meaningfulness of the question about life is based upon the assumption that life is just a combustion process[7]

---

[5] Frankl, HB, 664.

[6] Cf. Frankl, "On Logotherapy and Existential Analysis," *American Journal of Psychoanalysis*, 18, pp. 28-37, 1958.

[7] Cf. Frankl, DS, 31.

and therefore to ask its meaning is like demanding the meaning of a drop of water. He overlooks the fact that the drop of water may have a great weight of meaning to a thirsty materialist. At any rate, the positivist assigns to it the contemporary scientific curse, "metaphysical!" and hurriedly clears the floor for "important questions." The question of life's meaning is ignored by those who are so drugged by involvement in present aimless activity, as well as by those who, having already asked for it, but finding no answer, attempt to fill up the emptiness of life with the solace of drink or drugs.

Attempts to avoid posing the question of the meaning of life, and the ensuing responsibility of life, through such escapisms are always futile, however, for the answer is necessary for existence.

It is the task of the logotherapist to assist those who do pose the question, and fail to find a satisfactory answer. Frankl believes that this can be accomplished by virtue of the uniqueness and singularity of the individual.

At what seems to many to be the most vulnerable area, the transitoriness of life, Logotherapy finds human existence replete with meaning. The passing of time, rather than making life aimless, gives it its direction. It does not signify the passing of opportunity, but rather its presence. Instead of being lost in the past, an accomplishment is preserved by the past. Time can be a thief, it is true, but it can also be a trustee, who carefully guards the joy of meaningful tasks fulfilled. The pessimist who mourns the dwindling away of the pages of the wall calendar, could just as easily rejoice as he jots down the experiences of each day on its appropriate page and carefully stacks it away for future reference. The old man can rather rejoice in his treasure store of the past, than to envy the youth with his vital but unused talents.[8]

Thus the passing of life, in Logotherapy, becomes a focal point of meaning, rather than meaningless flux. Value potentials are secured forever by their present realization and committal to the past. The responsibility to realize these values makes of life a mission.

The meaning of life is also discovered in the conscience. This individual moral law gives an immediate basis for meaning. The transcendent demands of this immanent ethical impulse are the most certain of our experiences. As the saying goes, "the most certain science is conscience." Though one cannot see the law giver behind this moral law, yet it in itself intuitively certifies meaningfulness and responsibility to man.

Frankl sees meaning and responsibility also entailed in the objectivity of esthetic, as well as moral values. He believes that the experienced esthetic relativity is merely due to the subjective condition of the experiencer, and no proof of ethical relativity. "The realm of values is a transcendent realm of objective objects, for a value is necessarily transcendent of the act which intends it."[9] The world of values will always be viewed only in part and only from the unique perspective of the viewer, but neither its absoluteness nor its objectivity is thereby destroyed.

In addition to temporal, ethical, and esthetic experiences, life's meaning may be found in the very uniqueness of the individual. The most wretched existence has potential value. There are achievements of worth which only he can perform. Because of this, Frankl believes that euthanasia should never be a live option, and that self destruction can be pre-

---

[8] Cf. Frankl, DS, 38-39.
[9] Frankl, AS, 31.

sented as meaningless to the depressed patient. Frankl says that sweeping all the pieces off the board is not the way to solve a chess problem! Logotherapists try to challenge the despairing person to keep working at the problem. To try is a value in itself. "The rules of the game do not require us to win at all costs, but they do demand that we never give up the fight."[10]

Frankl cites the case of the apparently hopeless Negro convict being shipped from Marseilles to Devil's Island for life imprisonment. On the way, the ship caught fire, and the convict, a powerful man, was able to save the lives of ten men. For his heroic action, he was subsequently rewarded with a pardon. "Nobody knows whether he has yet something to expect from life, and what great hour perhaps yet waits for him."[11]

The important thing in the encounter with the person trying to find a meaning for his life, is to indicate for him a task. Since the therapist does not know what the patient should do, he, therefore, must not impose a task upon him. This does not make the problem insoluble, however, for the life task will present itself, and the person will be converted from patient (*patiens*) to agent (*agens*) when the decision is made to perform it. The patient will discover that the meaning was obscured by too much reflection upon the past or the future, rather than the present, the only possible temporal sphere of decision and achievement. A famous statement of Goethe sets forth this point clearly: How can we learn to know ourselves? Never by reflection but by action. Try to do your duty and you will soon find out what you are. But what is your duty? The demands of each day.

10 Frankl, DS, 60.
11 Frankl, AS, 45.

The question itself: What does life offer for me? should be radically criticized, according to logotherapeutic teaching, for it is wrongly put. The inquiry should really be as to what life demands of the individual. "It is life itself which puts the question to man. He is not to ask but rather to be asked. He has to answer (*antworten*) to life, he has to respond (*verantworten*) to life."[12] This responsibility comes through the call of conscience, which is also an answer. The religious man can appreciate this undeniable phenomenal fact better, for he realizes that "in the dialogue with his conscience, in this most intimate monologue, God is his partner."[13]

2. THE MEANING OF DEATH

Since Freud presented the death instinct as a basic drive of personality, there has been a good deal of effort put forth to understand the psychology of death, and to soften the traumatic pressure of its inevitable approach. Freud himself, however, left the topic more or less to others, while he developed in great detail the many ramifications of libido, the life instinct.

In Logotherapy the question of death is very pertinent. If the human personality is motivated by the will to meaning, how can this meaning be sustained in the light of the termination of existence? Is not that meaningless, which is eventually destroyed?

Frankl believes that, in a real sense, meaning is sustained by mortality. If one were eternal, then everything could be "put off until tomorrow," and meaning and values might never be realized. He asserts that the uncertainty of life is a stimulant to action, and a valuable aspect of human exist-

---

ence. "So in the face of death, as the insurmountable boundary of our future, and the limitation of our possibilities, we stand under the compulsion to utilize our lifetime, and not neglect the passing opportunities, whose finite sum represents one's total life."[14]

Logotherapy teaches life should be viewed as the raw material of a sculptor who does not know at which time he must stop working. Every day should be reckoned as if it were the last. The "irreversible character" of life is like a film from which no scenes may be "cut." The logotherapeutic "categorical imperative" is: "Act as if you were living for the second time and had acted as wrongly the first time as you are about to act now."[15]

The length of life has no bearing on its meaning. If life is meaningful, then quantity is not relevant. A book is not judged by the number of pages in it,[16] but rather, in the quality of its contents. A life which ends in its prime, may well be the most valuable, so long as it was characterized by primary concerns.

By the same token, the presence or absence of children is also irrelevant. If a life has no value in itself, it will not be redeemed by offspring. Each existence is an individual center, and will not be the more, or the less, meaningful by virtue of the physiological ability to reproduce. If life is not meaningful in itself, perpetuation will not give it meaning either. "Vital instinct satisfaction and biological procreation are only two sides of marriage, and not the most essential. The psychic moment of joyful love, or the spiritual moment of fellowship, is more essential."[17]

---

[14] Frankl, AS, 50.
[15] Frankl, DS, 73.
[16] Cf. Frankl, DS,
[17] Frankl, AS, 54.

Frankl sees in death a loss of the psychophysicum and self-consciousness. All that remains is the spiritual self. "Man has after death, no more ego, he 'has' nothing anymore, now he just 'is.' . . . Instead of being able to observe his life as a film, he becomes, in a sense, the film itself."[18] He becomes, respectively, his own heaven and his own hell. The paradox of death is that a man's past becomes the real future that he, during his life, awaited.

Thus to die is to become fulfilled and not something to be feared. The average man has a false idea of the passing of time, "he sees only the stubblefield of the past, but he overlooks the full granary of the past."[19] To die is to leave the transitoriness of time, and to become eternalized; paradoxically, death brings immortality.

Finitude and death are basic aspects of human existence. The person who is able to understand and bear this responsibility, as well as the responsibility of life, will to a great extent fulfill his existential potentialities. Logotherapy sees an opportunity for realizing some of the greatest attitudinal values in the moment of death.

3. THE MEANING OF LOVE[20]

The experience of love is, from the viewpoint of Logotherapy, one of the most significant existential events. A person validates himself through active creative tasks, but he may also do so passively through being loved. In the sense that every person yearns to be loved, and such a desire occupies so many of his thoughts and decisions, it may well be said that, "love makes the world go around."

---

[18] Frankl, ZV, 25.
[19] Frankl, HP, 70.
[20] Cf. Frankl, DS,

Love may be viewed in terms of three progressive phases; each being more authentic than the previous one. The first is sexuality. This is a commitment only to the body of another person and is not true love. If a person stops at this point, he will be destined for frustration, for sexuality, exclusively, will not satisfy the spirit.

The next phase is eroticism. This penetrates to the psyche of a person, but does not comprehend the personality. It is also transitory, being neither mature nor stable. This phase is commonly called infatuation.

True love is a commitment to the true center of personality, the "heart," the spiritual dimension. "Love is living the experience of another person in all its uniqueness, and singularity."[21] It involves "grace," "enchantment," and often a "miracle."

The grace is the unearned reciprocation of the beloved. This is neither a response due to the merit of the lover, nor a possession of the lover. Jealousy, therefore, represents something less than true love. The lover who is jealous considers that he "owns" the beloved, rather than that he, in the identification of love, "is" the beloved.

The enchantment is caused by the deep emotional experiences which come from the heart of the person in love. The miracle is the wonder of procreation.

Frankl believes that true love is eternal. Neither advancing age, physical deterioration, nor death can effect the relationship. He cites[22] a case in which cosmetic surgery to restore sagging breasts tended to endanger the relationship of a man and his wife, instead of strengthening it. "It is somehow no longer my wife." This demonstrates that love is independent

---

[21] Frankl, DS, 149.
[22] Cf. Frankl, AS, 109.

of physical change, and yet, somehow, also dependent upon it. The experience of love is, according to Logotherapy, no more disrupted by death than it is by distance, for the essence of love is that the lover is always near.

True love is, by the very nature of its participants, both necessarily monogamous and exclusive.[23] It is a spiritual act, a movement toward the highest possible value of the beloved person.[24]

Love of one's fellow men, and love of patients, is an important spiritual task of the psychotherapist. This is not such a deep or comprehensive commitment as love in courtship and marriage, nor does it include physical union as a factor. It is essential for the medical ministry in order to enable the physician to meet the existential needs of his patients. Rapport is only possible through love.

Frankl believes that most problems in the experience of love are based upon false "erotic materialism," which holds the superficial phases of love to be the most important. The therapist will have many opportunities to attempt to restore the proper value order, in this contemporary culture in which such a high premium is placed upon sex and sexual symbols.

4. The Meaning of Work

A meaningful life generally includes an occupation. This occupation must be considered a calling, a true vocation, however, if it is to satisfy the human being. He must sense that his task is somehow correspondent to his unique talents, and can only be properly fulfilled by him.

The high incidence of neuroses related to vocational problems in modern times appears to be due to the increasing im-

---

[23] Cf. O. Schwarz, *Psychology of Sex*, Penguin Books, 1949.

[24] Cf. M. Scheler, *Der Formalismus in der Ethik und die materiale Wertethik*, Niemeyer-Halle, 1921.

personality of industrial manufacture in its assembly lines,
and automation. Personal creativity is thwarted in a complex
production in which there is no apparent completion of useful commodities. This situation tends to create existential
frustration and existential vacuum as the spiritual dimension
in man is prevented from expressing itself vocationally.

In addition, periods of unemployment increase the apathy
and emptiness to such a degree that Frankl was motivated to
develop the concept of "unemployment neuroses." To this
point, however, the function of vocational creative values
must be put in the right perspective for the patient. We must
carefully differentiate between a neurotic attitude, which sees
work as the *sine qua non* of existence, and the proper attitude,
which considers work as a means to the end of meaningful
living.[25]

Another major problem in this area is also increasing at a
staggering pace. This is the so-called "pensioner's neurosis,"
whereby a forced retirement has stifled the creative urge in
human personality. Especially where the individual was "lost"
in his work, and found value only in incessant activity, is
this prevalent. Early indications of such problems may be
observed in the "Sunday neuroses" of those who are frustrated by the existential vacuum created by the cessation of
work for the weekend.

The logotherapist attempts to guide the patient to see the
possibility of creative values and meaningfulness in what
seem to be the most impersonal, or insignificant, tasks. The
personal commitment to them as a divine calling endues
them with both a valuable and a personal character. The
therapist also, however, must emphasize the importance of
experiential and attitudinal values, which may be realized,

---

[25] Cf. Frankl, DS, 144.

and may, more than creative values, fulfill the possibilities
of personality development, when vocational opportunities
are lacking.

B. *The Meaning of Suffering*

A major emphasis in Logotherapy is the attention given
to the misery of man. When opportunities of work are absent, failure is present, or the beloved does not reciprocate,
a life full of meaning is still possible. "Human life can be
fulfilled not only in creating and enjoying, but also in
suffering."[26]

Frankl has in mind here, of course, only that suffering
which is unavoidable. The masochistic desire for pain, and
the consequences of silly choices, do not provide value potentials in themselves. Only when a man's destiny brings about
unalterable circumstances in which despair arises does he
experience truly meaningful suffering. Even in the unavoidable circumstances, such as a malignancy beyond the ken and
competence of medicine, an untreatable physical defect, or
the imminence of death, however, there are opportunities to
experience some of the most important existential values,
attitudinal values.

It is not only the physician's task to help the patient to
attain a restoration of health in the psychophysicum, but
also, to minister to his spiritual needs. One of these great
needs, which one most often encounters among the ill and
helpless, is the need to be able to bear up under much suffering. "We no longer stand where classical psychotherapy
stands; we no longer view the task of psychotherapy to make
men merely able to work and, beyond that, able to enjoy

---

[26] Frankl, DS, 122.

themselves: at least to the same degree we must also make them capable of suffering."[27]

The problem of the suffering man is not so much the physical pain and the psychological pressure, as it is the absence of meaning in these experiences. Job was not so much tormented by his fate, as by the question why his fate had been thus. Nietzsche poses the question well: But it is not suffering in itself that is the problem, but rather the answer to the question "Why suffer?" is missing.

Logotherapy seeks to help the patient discover the answer to this question of the meaning of suffering. A case from the logotherapeutic clinic will illustrate this:

"A nurse of my clinic underwent a laparotomy which revealed an inoperable malignant tumor. In her despair, she called for me. In our discussion, it turned out that she was not so much in despair with respect to her illness, as in regard to her inability to go back to work. She loved her vocation above everything, and now was unable to perform it! What could I say to her in this situation? The situation of this nurse was really hopeless (she died one week later). However, I attempted to make it clear to her that to work eight or more hours in a day is no accomplishment, anyone can do that; but to be so willing to work as she was, and yet to be unable to do so, and, nevertheless, not to despair, that is a real achievement which few are able to carry out. So I asked her whether she would not be invalidating the service to thousands of patients, which she, as a nurse, had given, if she acted as if being ill had no meaning. As soon as she despaired in her situation, I told her, she made the meaning of a human life stand and fall upon how many hours a person works; and thus denied the ill and diseased every right

---

[27] Frankl, HP, 9.

to live, and every qualification for existence. In reality, she had been given a unique opportunity, inasmuch as all her previous service to those who placed their trust in her was professional aid, to do much more, to be an example of a true human being."[28]

As in the case of this nurse, despair is always the absolutizing of a particular, and, hence, relative value. The elevation of items in our environment, or our experience, to absolutes is destined for suffering. "Anyone who is in despair, thereby betrays the fact that he had idolized something."[29] This is, of course, not to say that every such absolutizing of relative values leads to neurosis (which is contended by Caruso, cf. page 82 above), for not all despair is pathological. However, it often is a part of neurotic pathology, and, even more often, drives a person to the doctor's office.

The ability to suffer is nothing more, or less, than the ability to realize attitudinal values. In a culture in which such a premium is placed upon material possessions, and physical achievement, it is sometimes difficult to reorient the patient to a true picture of man, meaning, and values. *Homo sapiens* is just as significant as *homo patiens*, as he is when expressed as *homo faber* or *homo amans*.[30]

A materialistic milieu honors the successful man, and bases its ethical judgments upon the line connecting the categories of success and failure. Frankl believes that a more important dimension is needed, however, which will fill out the sphere of personal achievement. This consists of the categories of fulfillment and despair which make allowance for the importance of one's attitude toward life. "Lack of success does not signify lack of meaning."[31] These facts are indicated by Frankl when he says that the dimension in which *homo patiens* moves (between the positive pole of fulfillment through suffering, and the negative pole of despair because of suffering) is perpendicular to the plane within which *homo faber* moves (between the positive pole of success and the negative pole of failure). From this perspective, failure is just as compatible with achievement as is success. It may be readily observed, on the other hand, that success in task achievement may also often be accompanied by despair. Upon investigation, one discovers that suicide is no respecter of persons; the rich are as susceptible as the poor.

The logotherapist's task, to enable the sufferer to accept his fate, and, thus to realize attitudinal values, is not easy, for it is nonsense to the spirit of the times. "In the eyes of *homo faber* the triumph of *homo patiens* must be foolishness and a stumbling block."[32] It requires love and patience, and a deep conviction that life's meaning is deeper than any circumstance. Any competent surgeon may amputate a leg, but it takes a man with personal assurance that suffering has a meaning, to show a despairing amputee that the meaning of life can never be dependent upon whether one goes about on one leg or two.[33]

So it becomes evident that upright, or "victorious," suffering is not only a real achievement in itself, but also is an important factor of growth and maturation of personality. The man who has learned to accept suffering has really become a man. He becomes enriched with personality traits which he could never have otherwise attained. A human being, therefore, according to Logotherapy, has a right to his own suffer-

---

[31] Frankl, DS, 123.
[32] Frankl, TT, 138.
[33] Cf. Frankl, DS, 278-9.

ing, and physicians must be careful that they do not deprive the patient of this right through indiscriminate use of tranquilizing medication.

The two great commandments of the doctor should be to "help where possible" and "soothe where necessary."[34] The alleviation of pain at "any price" is too often the basis of existentially crippling operations of the central nervous system, deep narcotic euphoria, or "careful neglect" in order to more quickly terminate an incurable illness. Every argument in behalf of euthanasia crumbles before the dignity of man and the existential analysis of suffering.

The doctor has a duty to prolong life, and the patient has a right to realize every value potential in it, even the value of the suffering which cannot be alleviated short of "quenching the spirit." "The intersection of the curves of these two above-mentioned commandments is very difficult to determine. The physician can only guess at which point the possibility of help merges into the necessity of alleviation. There is no law to help him, no rule to show the way. He can only choose according to his best knowledge and conscience. As he decides, he must do it by himself, and with his God, whose mandate is the conscience."[35]

The value in suffering, however, cannot be realized as a nihilistic act. Man can only have "confident despair" when he sees a ground for his confidence. He can bear his burdens only if there is essential meaning to counterbalance their distressing weight. "I can only intend suffering, I can only suffer meaningfully, when I have something, or someone, for whose sake I suffer."[36]

---

[34] Cf. Frankl, HP, 75 ff.

[35] Frankl, HP, 77-78.

[36] Frankl, HP, 69.

Suffering conceived as a sacrificial act for the sake of a loved one is pregnant with meaning. The logotherapist takes every opportunity to direct the despairing person to this possibility of meaning. Then an individual may even be thankful, may even rightly rejoice in his suffering.

A clinical case will demonstrate this possibility:

"An old practitioner came for treatment. A year before his beloved wife had died, and he could not overcome the loss. We asked this very despondent person whether he had considered what would have happened if he had died before his wife. 'There is no doubt about it,' he answered, 'she would have certainly been broken up.' Now we needed only to bring this to his attention, 'See here, your wife has been spared this, and you have saved her from it; the price is that now you must mourn her.' In the same moment his suffering had taken on meaning, the meaning of sacrifice, and he himself, the bereaved, was thereby comforted."[37]

For the religious person there is an even higher reference of sacrificial life in God. The final answer to the question of suffering which Nietzsche presented can be grounded only in what Frankl calls the "suprameaning" of life, a concept of his which we may certainly identify with a "religious meaning," inasmuch as Frankl himself has pointed out the similarity of his concept with "Providence."[38] The non-religious man can only face the fact that it is the suffering of fate which is in a position to ask him the question, and not vice versa. He must answer, and he must pass the test. If life has a meaning in any of its phases, then it must certainly have meaning in the great existential crises of suffering. Frankl is convinced that here the greatest existential values are realized, here are forged the treasures that make life worth living. Suffering can

---

[37] Frankl, TT, 137-138.
[38] Cf. Frankl, HP, 112.

only be understood in reference to something beyond the suffering man. "The calculation of human suffering can be computed only in Transcendence; in immanence it remains an open question."[39]

We shall now turn to a discussion of transcendence, and the religious dimension of personality in the psychotherapeutic setting.

C. *Logotherapy and Religion*

Logotherapy is a religiously oriented theory. It is in full agreement with Einstein that "science without religion is lame, religion without science is blind."[40] It posits a spiritual unconscious which is more important than the psychic unconscious, which Freud so effectively impressed upon the twentieth century. The repression of these unconscious spiritual impulses is held to be more destructive in the personality development of modern man than the stifling of his instinctive psychic drives. The bringing to consciousness of the spiritual factors of human existing, along with the entailed responsibilities, is the prime function of Logotherapeutic practice. These considerations lead us to the question of the relationship between Logotherapy and the religious life of the patient. What are the specific goals of the medical ministry of Logotherapy?

This is an important question, the answer of which was a chief stimulus for the undertaking of this brief excursion through the literature, and practice, of Frankl's Existential Analysis.

---

[39] Frankl, HP, 115.
[40] Einstein, Albert, *Out of My Later Years,* Philosophical Library, p. 26.

The entrance into psychotherapeutic practice of those problems and crises which were formerly considered the jurisdiction of the priest or pastor, has not been a matter of choice. Persons, having grown up in an era whose spirit has been secularistic, seem naturally to look to a scientist for help. It may also be true that they feel more secure before an in· dividual who is experienced in keeping confidences, rather than one, such as the minister, who is, at least proverbially, noted for giving condemnation. At any rate, there is present truth in what Kierkegaard said more than a century ago: "Ministers are no longer caretakers of the soul; physicians do it now."[41]

Although most contemporary therapists are more cordial to religious impulses in their patients than was the case a few years ago, there still remains the specter of suspicion that these impulses may well be symptoms of pathological processes. "Most analysts would question the results of their therapy in a patient who persisted in his religious practices at the end of an analysis."[42] Even those who do not consciously disparage religious values, often do so unconsciously. An anthropological perspective based upon automatically functioning, instinctive drives is rooted in a philosophy which has been historically anti-religious. "Psychodynamic psychiatry threatens the strict religious dogmas. It seems to do this by its implicit values rather than by explicit statement."[43]

Logotherapy, however, neither avoids dealing with man's religious experiences, nor reduces them to mechanistic drives. Any psychotherapy which involves values (and what therapy

---

[41] Cited from Frankl, TT, 116.

[42] Ginsburg, and Herma, *American Journal of Psychotherapy*, 7, 546, 1953.

[43] Redlich, F., *American Journal of Psychiatry*, Vol. 114, p. 800, 1958.

can avoid them?) must be prepared to deal with the religious problems that are connected with these values. Instead of deploring such an obligation, Frankl asserts that it may lead to real satisfaction in the patient's life, and signal success in the therapeutic practice. Existential Analysis is designed to uncover the unconscious religious facet of personality, while Logotherapy, in the technical sense, meets the problems arising from this new emergence in the patient's experience. "The object of Existential Analysis is unconscious faith, the object of Logotherapy is conscious unbelief."[44]

The authority of the psychotherapist to enter into the religious sphere of personality is widely disputed, but the logotherapist insists that such resistance to dealing with the patient as a "whole" person in his "physical-psychological-spiritual totality" is neither possible nor sensible. "Both Existential Analysis and Logotherapy have not only the right, but rather also the duty to deal with such questions, and upon a simple ground: already in the area of their psychotherapeutic sphere of treatment, religious problems are necessarily thrust upon them."[45] It is the intention of Logotherapy to meet these problems consciously and confidently.

On the other hand, Frankl is insistent that Logotherapy is not a religious system per se. It neither aims to preach or to moralize, but rather to deal with the problems of meaning and value. It is not a system of ethics, but merely deals with the fact that man is an ethical being. The boundaries between psychotherapy and religion must be strictly observed, and trespassing from one area to the other is strictly forbidden.

[44] Frankl, HP, 102.
[45] Frankl, HP, 102.

The minister and the therapist have two different vocational tasks. Frankl maintains that the psychotherapist is dedicated to the "healing of the soul" (*seelische Heilung*), while the minister is assigned to the "saving of the soul" (*Seelenheil*). It sometimes occurs that the intention of one sphere becomes an effect, a side-effect, of the other, but this should always be *per effectum* and not *per intentionem*. "The German author, J. H. Schultz, rightly warns psychotherapists, including analysts, not to set themselves up as peddlers in philosophy, as moralists, as pastor substitutes, or as schoolmasters."[46] The therapist is not "called" to give a religious answer to his patient's religious quest, but rather must remain strictly neutral.

Frankl believes that the "medical ministry" must not become a "handmaid to theology," for this would be of benefit to neither area. He states this in opposition to Caruso's claim that psychotherapy should be an *ancilla theologiae,* just as scholastics had demanded of philosophy. Scientific psychotherapy would be deprived of its right of free inquiry and research, which would hinder its progress. Theology, on the other hand, would lose the advantages that accrue from "the material of independent research which may place useful arguments into the hands of theology,"[47] It might also be led, thereby, into the pitfall of degrading itself by the presumption that the purpose of worshipping God is in order to obtain good mental health.

The therapist and the minister should cooperate, but they should not engage in interdisciplinary activity as a vocational function. "When the physician meets the patient on the same confessional ground and then deals with him in a sort

---

[46] Vander Veldt and Odenwald, *Psychiatry and Catholicism,* McGraw-Hill, New York, 1957, p. 206.
[47] Frankl, MS, 57.

of personal union, then he has ceased treating his patient as a physician."[48] Even if the therapist is also trained in a religious vocation, he must decide in which sphere he will deal with the patient so as not to confuse the two different vocational goals. Frankl emphasizes that irreligious persons, or those of a different confessional group, must always be met with complete tolerance by such religiously oriented therapists. Logotherapy considers itself as a scientific discipline which investigates and treats human beings even in their religious dimension of life. It is not a religious treatment however, and remains neutral to specific religious commitments. Frankl feels that, as a science, it must remain "open" to all religious systems, which he thinks are forming the next higher dimension, i.e., the dimension of the suprahuman.

Though Logotherapy is dedicated to the task of realizing meaning and values, it is also dedicated against the imposition of meaning and values upon the patient. "The physician must guard against any imposition of a world view, his world view. A transference (or, better said, counter-transference) of a personal world view, his own value system, upon the patient is not permitted."[49]

Any true religious response must be existential, the free choice and spontaneous commitment of an individual. "True religiosity comes neither by the instinctual drives of the id, nor by the pressure of the physician."[50] Both religious impulse and direction can be left to the choice of the patient. The therapist need only to indicate their presence in the patient's personality and their potentiality for the meaning of his life.

---

[48] Frankl, MS, 56.
[49] Frankl, TT, 119.
[50] Frankl, UG, 111.

The patient may be challenged in terms of religious goals, but, according to Logotherapy, his personality must not be violated by the challenge to any specific religious goals. Dr. Weisskopf-Joelson of Purdue University, an admirer of Logotherapy, seems to go beyond such a general challenge: "Psychoanalytic thinking is based upon the assumption that the successfully analyzed patient will automatically develop his own philosophy of life, or he will avail himself of a ready-made philosophy which is available in his culture. This assumption becomes more tenuous if the culture offers little by way of such philosophies. . . . Lack of strong comprehensive and consistent faith characterizes the entire world at the present time. Thus synthesis, following psychological analysis, cannot be left to chance."[51] Frankl would retort that it is true that the synthesis must not be left to *chance,* it must rather, be left to the *patient.*

The process of the medical ministry of Logotherapy is not to give values, but rather, to bring to the consciousness of the patient both the need for values, and the unconscious spiritual values within his own personality. Frankl believes that when a patient is sensitive to his conscience, he will have revealed to him the personal values and meaning which he should realize in his life. Logotherapy seeks to "stir up" this underlying value potential, and not to invade the personality with a value system.

Thus Logotherapy utilizes the immanent potentialities of human nature, and also leads the patient to the boundary of Transcendence wherein he may find the ground of meaning for his life. Here will be found, if at all, the rationale for his life's responsibilities, and the strength for his suffering.

---

[51] Weisskopf-Joelson, "Logotherapy and Existential Analysis," *Acta Psychotherapeutica,* Vol. 16, No. 3 (1958), p. 202.

However, Logotherapy can only lead the patient to the door of Transcendence. He must enter by himself. A scientific therapy, grounded in empirical and phenomenological data, can, and should in Frankl's opinion, go no further. An adequate therapy, however, should go at least that far. To neglect the true spiritual nature of man, and to neglect his transcendent reference, is to fail in the true vocation of therapy. Logotherapy not only recognizes this dimension of personality, but also, commits itself, in its medical ministry, to a comprehensive therapy for the "complete man."

This concludes our exposition of Frankl's existential psychotherapy, known as Logotherapy. Such a brief survey will, of necessity, omit important facets of this psychiatric theory and therapy which is comprehended by a wide and growing body of literature, as well as a wide area of clinical application. It remains yet to ask the question: What shall one think of Logotherapy? Inasmuch as the research of this volume was undertaken to answer a personal inquiry as to the meaning and value of Logotherapy for the biblically oriented Christian therapist, the answer to the above question will be largely restricted to this end. For the answer, we shall proceed to the concluding chapter.

CHAPTER VII

LOGOTHERAPY
AND THE CHRISTIAN THERAPIST

We live in an age in which the macrocosm of the universe and the microcosm of the atom are rapidly revealing their long kept secrets to the inquisitive and persistent search of the modern scientist. Another microcosmic entity, however, the human personality, has been more successful in resisting the scientific inquiry, and paradoxically, with every revelation it becomes more inscrutable. Whereas so many persons are, in spite of the dramatic progress of twentieth century technology, hounded by the age-old problems of fear and personal defeat, it is a pressing demand upon those who labor in the field of mental hygiene to discover the nature of man, and thereby, hopefully, find the means to meet his needs.

There is reason to believe that much of the difficulty has not been so much due to the nature of the object, the individual, as to the method of inquiry. When viewed as a material complex or a biological specimen, volumes of data may be obtained, but the more precise and penetrating the observations, the more irrelevant they seem to be to man as a human being. It may well be that progress in this area is dependent upon a new perspective.

An old, and in modern times little considered, point of view is becoming more prominent in the contemporary scene. It is that the essence of man is not to be discovered as a material or psychological mechanism, but only through a transcendent point of reference. Man is a spiritual, existential entity whose problems will only be properly understood and dealt with when his true religious characteristics are brought to the focus of attention. The secret of man is that he is made after the image of God!

This approach has stimulated, in recent days, a concerted effort to correlate the fields of psychotherapy and religion, in order to adapt the healing techniques of psychological science to the transcendent character of man. Logotherapy has been developed with a careful regard for the limitations of each discipline, and with the hope that it will "stand in the gap" and encounter successfully the crises of modern man.

The first impression of Logotherapy is certainly very positive. Here is a theory which is philosophically alert and, in practical application, therapeutically effective. It concerns itself with the unique existential character of the human being and yet recognizes its primary task in the psychotherapeutic encounter with particular persons beset by concrete problems. It not only criticizes the foibles of modern psychiatry, but also offers a positive program to rectify them. Logotherapy, at least in its initial presentation, appears to be a "haven in a time of storm."

Inasmuch as the author is convinced that the Christian philosophy of life is that which truly comprehends reality, it is a matter of personal importance to ascertain the validity of

Logotherapy in the light of his presuppositions. This may seem to be a rather narrow base of judgment, but, in this sense, philosophical presuppositions are either "narrow," that is to say, precise and exclusive, or else a hopeless hodgepodge of loose thinking. The person who denies having presuppositions from which he bases all of his critical judgments, is either embarrassed by the latter, or ashamed of the former. He may try to hide behind the title "scientist," but, in his evaluations, he will be a philosopher, whether he wants to or not, and for weal or for woe.

The Christian world view, upon which the evaluation of Logotherapy is to be made, is based upon the biblical revelation as the Word of God. It has been unfolded historically through the Hebrew-Christian tradition, and presents itself as the criterion of meaning and value for man through all the ages. This thesis, which is, of course, a commitment of faith (as is every philosophy, every judgment, and hence, all knowledge) will not be here supported by an accompanying apologetic argument, but rather, is presented in order that the reader will understand the use of the term "Christian." It is not an "official" world view, but instead, is the product of the author's experience and the fruit of his study of the Scriptures. Thus, though he believes that God has revealed Himself through an infallible Word, it is far from his mind to claim an infallible understanding of it.

Logotherapy will be considered first in reference to its clinical usefulness, and then with respect to its adaptability for the Christian therapist. This is not intended to be an exhaustive critique, but rather, merely suggestive of the reaction of the author following a rather intensive study of Logotherapy in its literature and in its clinical application.

A. *Logotherapy as a Clinical Tool*

Although the major concern of this chapter is the specific relationship between Logotherapy and the Christian faith, it is well to indicate some of the areas of difficulty that one may find in the logotherapeutic theory and diagnosis of mental illness. These problems are significant for the clinician in general, for, of course, there is no specific biblical view of differential diagnosis as such, or of any specific technique of treatment.

The diagnostic schema of Logotherapy will probably be more suggestive than convincing to the average American therapist. The theory of relating illness to both etiology and symptomatology is, to be sure, a necessity in the purview of a comprehensive medical theory, but it is nevertheless true that the practice of diagnosis is almost exclusively symptomatological. The etiology is usually derived as an inference from the symptoms, along with the reevaluation from the result of treatment. In addition, the logotherapeutic schema (cf. page 76) with its four categories, does not contain a place for the pseudo-neuroses, and thus a major diagnostic category is excluded. They are obviously not psychoses, yet, being described as somatogenic with psychic symptoms, they would fall under the definition for psychoses. Frankl himself is fully aware of this difficulty. He says[1] that in (pseudo-) neurotic cases, we have to deal with a "micropsychic" symptomatology and a "microsomatic" etiology. Moreover, his schema was constructed to serve didactic purposes, and so to be of merely heuristic value. Nevertheless, both the diagnostic schema, and this particular nosological category of pseudo-neurosis, are presented as being significant in logotherapeutic

---

[1] Frankl, TT, 48.

teachings; and are mutually exclusive. The laws of logic dictate that one or both be changed.

In addition, the defining of psychoses as somatogenic will seem to be a bit premature in the case of the functional psychoses. It is true that psychotherapeutic treatment has been relatively ineffective in the treatment of endogenous depression, schizophrenia and paranoia, but it is also true that somatotherapy has been something less than a signal success with them. Certainly not enough to provide the evidence for a physical etiology. Studies in hematology, and other areas of biochemical research, are making considerable progress in the attempt to isolate somatic factors which are peculiar to functionally psychotic patients, but the demonstration of somatogenesis appears to be distant and/or dubious. It seems that such categorizing falls short of the logotherapeutic goal of positive diagnosis. It would, apparently, in this respect be better to suspend judgment until more evidence is available. Psychogenesis still appears to be a live option.

The discovery of the proper medication for the differential treatment of pseudo-neuroses, by Frankl, is a major step of progress in somatotherapy, but it is questionable whether it can yet be termed a causal therapy in view of the mysterious interrelation of the somatic and psychic dimensions. The effects upon the vegetative and endocrinal systems by emotional experience, and vice versa, is presently but a little known area of investigation.

In the area of the psychogenic problems and the different categories of reactive neuroses, Logotherapy does not seem to make enough allowance for historical causal factors. In the author's opinion, neuroses are usually rooted in early childhood traumatic, anxiety producing, experiences which have caused a defect in the personality development. Later, personal pressure, or, sometimes, the absence of pressure and conflict bring to consciousness the anxiety states of these early trauma. This anxiety, or objectless fear, often becomes objectified in phobic objects or compulsive acts, and then the phenomenon of anticipatory anxiety comes into play. It closes the neurotic circle by precipitating the feared state of affairs.

In this sense, anticipatory anxiety, rather than the causal factor, is the precipitating and sustaining factor of neurosis. Instead of being the etiological factor, anticipatory anxiety seems rather to lower the psychological "immunity" to neurosis to the point where a neurotic state comes to pass, much the same as an emotional state may "precipitate" a case of tuberculosis. It should be noted that the existential methods of Logotherapy, which cut across the neurotic circle through the utilization of psychonoetic antagonism, would be equally applicable to either theoretical description. In this point of view, however, the obvious relevance in most cases of the symptoms to early experiences is taken into account.

It also, perhaps, should be mentioned that in the psychiatric literature, and in the author's personal experience, the phobic reduction of anxiety does not appear to be channeled into such narrow categories as seem to be indicated in Logotherapy. On the contrary, the number and variety of phobic objects are almost as unlimited as the possible objects of experience. In every case, the attendant anxiety is felt as a sense of dread, an undefined threat to personal existence. To be sure, Frankl uses this "narrow categorizing" only in the cases of "reactive neuroses," and not for psychogenic neuroses, in general; however, when the reactive neuroses are subtracted from the general category of neuroses, in the strict sense of the word, there seems to be no remainder.

Though precise diagnosis is a worthy aim in any clinical activity, it is an ideal that is very difficult to attain. In psychotherapy, there are those who maintain that it is not an absolute necessity, but rather is in many cases irrelevant to an effective psychotherapeutic practice. A careful physical examination may help to isolate physical problems, but when the symptoms are confined to the psychic (and/or spiritual) dimension, it is not easy to make a decisive causal diagnosis or nosological decision. The usual "mixture" of the symptoms, and the uniqueness of them, not infrequently draws different diagnoses from equally competent therapists. Inasmuch as the psychotherapeutic application of Logotherapy is directed toward the patient's attitudes regarding his symptoms, the emphasis upon a differential diagnosis of the neuroses themselves, apart from the importance of discovering possible physical complications, seems to lack necessity.

The therapeutic method of paradoxical intention holds very great promise in the field of psychotherapy. Frankl appears to have certified it, by a great deal of careful case reports, as an adequate, versatile, and valid technique. On the other hand, the actual application and effectiveness of de-reflection is neither so clear nor so convincing as is the case with paradoxical intention. Certainly Frankl would point to the fact that de-reflection has to be followed by the actual application of Existential Analysis, i.e., an elucidation of those concrete meaning potentialities and life tasks in the patient's personal experience; regarding the technical aspects of such endeavors, however, one may hope that this technique will be more fully developed in the logotherapeutic literature, both theoretically and in its practical application, in the near future.

There seems to be an ambivalence in logotherapeutic teachings as to whether de-reflection is really a technique serving

Existential Analysis, as paradoxical intention serves Logotherapy (in the specific, narrow sense of the term), or
whether it is merely a term indicating the transfer of the
patient's attention from self-centeredness to objective values,
and thus not really a technique at all. It is, however, certainly presented as a specific therapeutic technique,[2] though
in a context from which it is difficult to extricate de-reflection
as distinct from paradoxical intention and/or existential analytic therapy. It is the author's contention that Frankl would
add considerable weight to both the theoretical and practical
aspects of his teaching, if he were to develop de-reflection as
a specific mode and means of the existential analytic phase.

The short term treatment of Logotherapy is one of its characteristics which will most interest the American clinician.
However, care should be exercised to avoid making the
length of therapy an end in itself. Extremely short term con-
tacts, which do not permit the full orbed personal relationship of the therapist with the patient, might unconsciously
cause the existential therapist to revert to the folly of an
impersonal, mechanical treatment in which the patient is
again a "thing," howbeit an existential thing.

Logotherapy, as a clinical theory and therapy of neuroses,
has the potential of giving a new hope and enthusiasm in
psychotherapeutic practice. Such hope and enthusiasm in the
personal outlook of the therapist is, in itself, a powerful component in establishing a truly therapeutic atmosphere. In addition, the appeal to the existential potential of the spiritual
dimension of the patient's personality may provide a "giant
step" in the progress of modern psychotherapy.

The above-mentioned problems, which the author finds in
his perusal of the various aspects of logotherapeutic teachings,

---

[2] Cf. Frankl, TT, 95 ff.

should not be permitted to obscure his essential agreement with the theory and therapy of neurosis in Logotherapy. Neither should the negative character of these criticisms be allowed to devaluate the very valuable contribution of Logotherapy to the "needs of the hour" in the field of mental health.

B. *Logotherapy and Biblical Anthropology*

It is immediately apparent that logotherapeutic anthropology has a close affinity to a Christian view of man. One is tempted to say *the* Christian view of man, but in the light of the wide differences of opinion as to how the biblical data should be systematized, the author must use his own interpretation in making a comparison. Thus it will be presented from the perspective of biblical data while bearing in mind that there is no precise unanimity regarding a Christian anthropology.

The anthropological, psychological concepts of the Bible, such as "soul," "spirit," "heart," and "mind," have no precise scientific definition, but rather must be understood from their contexts. For example, sometimes "soul" and "spirit" are used synonymously, sometimes distinctively, and sometimes antithetically. This problem is, of course, not exclusively biblical. The German transliteration of "soul," *Seele*, and its derivatives, frequently used in theological and psychological literature, has as wide, or perhaps even wider range of meaning than does the biblical term.

In terms of structure the logotherapeutic view of man is without difficulty coordinated with that of the Bible. The most apparent analogy is the view, emphasized in contemporary dispensational theology, which propounds a threefold structure of man, and which goes by the historically popular, but descriptively poor, title, "trichotomy" ("triunity" would be more pertinent). Care must always be exercised in "structuring" to keep in mind the essential unity of the human being.

The biblical view, while also emphasizing the unity of man, gives a substantive characteristic to the spiritual dimension, which enables man to be "absent from the body and present with the Lord." However, "discarnate" man is not "complete," and will not be truly man until the spirit is reconciled to a physical structure. Logotherapy would, perhaps, hesitate to grant such explicit substantiation to the spiritual dimension inasmuch as it may appear to threaten the unity of man.[3]

The logotherapeutic concept of the spirit very closely approximates the biblical concept of the heart. Out of the heart "flow the issues of life" as is the case of the spiritual unconscious. The heart also has a conscious facet in which existentially decisive activity originates — "if thou shalt believe in thine heart . . . thou shalt be saved." This core of personality, the biblical ego, can be found in many ways to be parallel to logotherapeutic anthropology.

In the Bible, the psychophysicum is also "factive" in relation to the "facultative" character of the spiritual dimension. Occasionally the term "body" is inclusive of the psyche, and sometimes the latter is referred to as "flesh" and sometimes as soul. The psychonoetic antagonism is manifested as the "spirit wars against the flesh." In the Bible the spiritual dimension is considered also constitutive of man and higher in significance, "fear not those that kill the body . . . fear him who is able to cast [you] into hell." However, the psychophysicum is, nevertheless, necessary for the whole man. Man

---

[3] Cf. Frankl, UM, 104 ff. for a discussion of the "substance" of the spiritual dimension.

is considered an essential unity and his body has no more, or no less, dignity than any other aspect of his personality.

The Bible is, of course, in no wise a revelation of systematic anthropology. It emphasizes, rather, throughout its teachings, that man is unique with respect to the rest of creation, that he is a spiritual creature, that he is made after the image of God. This image is not clearly detailed in the Scriptures, but it includes, at least, a unique potentiality of man to commune and have fellowship with God. Man is essentially religious. His kinship with the animal kingdom, by virtue of a similar psychophysical character, is incidental in the light of his kinship with God, through his spirituality. This gives him dignity, creativity, and, since it is a gift of God, responsibility.

Logotherapy is not a Christian anthropology in any technical sense, but it has the same basic emphases in its presentation. Here is an anthropological direction for which the Christian therapist may be truly thankful inasmuch as it presents a picture of man as an essentially spiritual existence, and from the setting of modern clinical psychiatry.

The phenomenological data of Logotherapy, which demonstrates that man is to be understood in terms of a transcendent reference point, is confirmatory of the explicit and implicit theses of the Bible, that man can be only understood in relation to his Creator.

The repudiation which Logotherapy undertakes, of the contemporary "head in the sand" scientism of much modern anthropology, will no doubt strengthen the hand of the Christian psychotherapist.

Frankl's anthropology, as an empirical description and existential analysis of man, is very helpful as a complement to the Christian view of man, ascertained from the Scriptures. While it appears doubtful whether phenomenology could ever bring one to the lawgiver behind the phenomenon of conscience, strictly from the phenomenal data, it is at this point that the Christian revelation is most specific. Jehovah God, revealed in Jesus Christ, is presented as the Creator and Sustainer of the universe, as well as the One who writes the "ten words" of the moral law of conscience upon the heart of man.

C. *Logotherapy and Motivation*

In reference to human motivation, one again finds a high degree of correlation between logotherapeutic and Christian perspectives. In Logotherapy, the "must" of the instinctive drives of psychodynamic psychology, and the "can" of the self-actualization theories of ego-psychology, give way to the "ought" of responsible existential decision. "Psychotherapy of today generally interprets that category of being which is called human being (*Dasein*) either in the sense of necessity or potentiality, of needs to be met or possibilities to be realized, of 'I must' or 'I can.' What is yet lacking is the additional interpretation of being in the sense of obligation."[4]

All goals of action for selfish, or self-centered, purposes are repudiated as true human objectives. Neither pleasurable satisfaction nor personal self-realization are accepted, in Logotherapy, as the proper basis for striving.

All egocentric motivational goals, whether for pleasurable, materialistic, or intellectual ends, are also condemned as futile in the Scriptures. In the Old Testament, the result of such attempted life patterns is couched in a phrase very similar to Frankl's "existential frustration," the "vexation of

---

[4] Frankl, "Logotherapy and the Challenge of Suffering," *Review of Existential Psychology and Psychiatry,* Vol. 1, No. 1, 1960.

spirit." This experience, the direct result of the individual's trying to secure self-centered goals, apart from the demands of responsibility in his spiritual dimension, is described as "vanity of vanities," which may be translated as the "greatest emptiness." This, in turn, brings to mind the logotherapeutic term, "existential vacuum." It should be stated, parenthetically, that the Bible does not deny (anymore than does Logotherapy) the dignity of the individual, nor the valid enjoyment of sensuous pleasure, but it does condemn primary motivation with these and other egocentric ends as goals.

Also for the Christian there is the necessity for grounding one's life in an objective realm of meaning and values. However, the Christian world and life view is very specific in terms of its value system. It affirms that God has revealed the true standard of values in the ten commandments of the moral law, and that these are binding upon all men everywhere. The moral consciousness, or conscience, brings to the awareness of man the demands of this moral system as it relates to any particular decision in a specific concrete situation. These ethical demands are explicitly stated in the Bible, and even those who are not cognizant of the biblical teaching are "without excuse," for this law is written "on their hearts." However, the conscience is liable to being "seared over as with a hot iron," and, therefore, may be culturally and socially conditioned, or repressed, to the extent that the moral law is not revealed with sufficient accuracy so as to enable the individual to make a proper moral choice.

From the Christian point of view there is an important factor which is not taken into account by Logotherapy, or at least is not sufficiently emphasized. The popular phrase, "will to meaning," which supersedes the "will to pleasure" and the "will to power," should, in turn, be supplemented by the "will to sin." It is a central aspect of biblical teaching, and one having abundant empirical evidence, that man has within him a negative motivation in reference to the dictates of his conscience. The Apostle Paul expresses it as being unable to do what one *should* do, and persisting in doing what one *should not*. This principle of sin, which is defined as a transgression of the moral law of God, cannot, from the Christian point of view, be accounted for either in terms of ignorance, or in human finitude preventing the realization of right choice, but, rather, is a positive inclination to resist the right choice.

Frankl is, of course, not unaware of the "problem of sin," and would, perhaps, be in qualified agreement. However, he would feel that this sin factor does not enter into the psychotherapeutic system of Logotherapy per se, inasmuch as the therapist must of necessity operate under the pragmatic "fiction" that every patient is a free and competent being having the requisite power to cooperate in a successful treatment. The Christian therapist also utilizes this pragmatic "fiction," but he keeps carefully in mind the practical "fact" of the great influence of sin upon the life and problems of the patient.

This factor obviously complicates the problem involved in challenging individuals to fulfill objective values. At least this is true for the Christian therapist, for he considers all values in a moral context. This is due to the fact that in a Christian *Weltanschauung* there is only one acceptable purpose in life, and that is to advance the Kingdom of Christ. A central concept of the Christian faith is that the principle of sinful, self-oriented striving, which is the obstacle to the realization of true meaning and values, is obviated only through a radical reorientation of the spirit, which, in turn, is contingent upon an act of personal trust and commitment, called faith, to the person and work of Christ. This radical reorientation, known as regeneration, is an immediate act of God, through the Holy Spirit of God dealing with the spirit of man.

With these essential characteristics, or reservations, in mind, the Christian may wholeheartedly agree with Frankl's repudiation of any self-oriented motivational goal, as well as with his emphatic assertion that normal adult motivation must be based upon the attempt to realize meaning and values in an objective world. This world is not to be considered as the objective projection of human personality, but rather, as the creation of a Transcendent Person, who assigns specific tasks for each man, according to the specific talents of each man, and which will, if fulfilled, be the optimum of realization of the individual.

Although Logotherapy is explicit about the function of anxiety in personality, and emphasizes the demand upon the individual to meet the responsibilities of life, there is no really satisfactory discussion of the place of guilt in the logotherapeutic practice. This is usually considered an important phase of existential psychology, and is of great significance in a biblical world view (as well as psychotherapeutic practice). "The condition of the individual when confronted with the issue of fulfilling his potentialities is *anxiety* . . . when the person denies these potentialities, fails to fulfill them, his condition is *guilt*."[5]

Frankl considers at length the responsibility of man, which he considers the central existential characteristic of human personality, and the possible neurotic problems which may be consequent to an ignoring of this obligation, but he gives little space to the consideration of the resultant despairing

---

[5] May, Rollo, et al, *Existence*. A New Dimension in Psychiatry and Psychology. Basic Books, Inc., New York, 1958, p. 52.

sense of guilt that is such a significant human experience.[6] In the Christian world view, true guilt is the consequence of disobeying God, the result of sinful choice. It is considered the divine warning to man of his failure to be responsible and should never be analyzed or psychologized away.

The distinction of true and false senses of guilt[7] is indeed a thorny problem. True guilt is a judgment of God through the conscience, and is an act of grace. False guilt is that which comes of the judgments of men and is a terrible frustrating burden. The therapist is, of course, not able to discriminate between these two in most cases, nor, fortunately, is it his task so to do. However, he must deal with them both as components of the personal despair of his patients.

Though it is true that the Christian therapist should not bring either inquiry or accusation of sin and guilt into the therapeutic encounter, he must have both clearly understood as components of human motivation. Few, if any, are the cases of human failure, confronting the therapist, which are free from these factors. It is an unrealistic therapeutic perspective, from the Christian point of view, which either does not have them clearly conceptualized in its anthropological thesis, or treats them as phenomena of immanent psychodynamic conflict.

---

[6] Frankl discusses guilt and repentance in HP, 74-5 (this passage is primarily concerned with showing the essential difference between masochism and martyrdom and/or penitence); ZV, F.n., 19-20; and "Sinndeutung des Leidens," *Jahresgabe des Schweizerischen Verbandes der Freunde der Hebräischen Universität Jerusalem an seine Mitglieder*, Zurich, 1957, p. 6. In a certain sense, Frankl sees sin and guilt as both more difficult and more superficial than the Christian point of view: more superficial in that it is not presented as being a significant factor of personality; more difficult because no real solution is seen beyond a hope of grace.

[7] Cf. Tournier, Paul, *Echtes und falsches Schuldefühl*, Rascher Verlag, Zürich, 1959.

Frankl, of course, is not unaware of the significance of guilt in the psychotherapeutic practice, and presents it as a basic human problem, "guilt feelings certainly play a great role in the psychology of obsessive-compulsive neurosis,"[8] but he does not, in the author's view, sufficiently consider it as a judgment of God, or its alleviation as being different from the alleviation of any psychodynamic problem. In Logotherapy, it is rightly asserted that "only a being which is responsible can become guilty,"[9] but the remedy for objective guilt, which derives from the failure before objective responsibility, is lacking.

The insistence of Logotherapy upon the realization of meaning and values in human striving as the proper goal of action is an emphasis that is sorely needed in modern psychotherapeutic circles. The Christian therapist will reap a harvest of benefits from this stress on directing the personality toward objective, rather than ego-centered goals. Herein lies true ego-satisfaction and self-development. However, he also will stand convinced that only that objectively oriented striving which is directed to the advancement of the Kingdom of God is non-ego-centered. Meaning and value are necessary goals of personality development, but only that meaning and value which is ordained of God.

D. *Logotherapy and Therapeutic Goals*

The aspect of Logotherapy that is most interesting, at least from the religious perspective, is that which goes beyond somatic problems, or the psychotherapeutic treatment of specific neurotic illnesses, and takes into account the spiritual dimension of man. The logotherapeutic thesis is that the person

[8] Frankl, TT, 114.
[9] Frankl, TT, 114.

must be challenged with meaningful goals when his life is crippled by the frustration of his existence. This brings one directly to the realm of religious values and the overall goal of the therapist.

Frankl believes that the medical ministry, though related to a realm of religious values, must be clearly distinguished, however, from the religious ministry. The former has as its primary aim the "healing of the soul," while the latter is properly directed toward the "saving of the soul." He grants that the primary aim of one discipline may become a result of the other discipline, or sphere, and vice versa, but warns against the confusing of intentions and effects, which would violate the distinction of the spheres.

The Christian therapist, however, as a member of a religious group which believes that it has a mandate to declare the claims of Christ to "every creature," which asserts the priesthood of every believer, and which recognizes no valid vocation which is not specifically oriented to the gospel of Christ, will apparently have to keep in mind the hope of the patient's salvation, as well as his psychic well being. These are, however, in themselves only secondary goals to the primary goal of glorifying God through Jesus Christ, which, in the last analysis, is the prime requisite of Christian discipleship.

From the perspective of Logotherapy, these tasks would be in two separate vocational spheres, whereas the biblical revelation, on the other hand, while recognizing a diversity of vocations, none of which has to do specifically with the process of salvation, or regeneration (an act of God), but all of which are involved in "bearing witness" to the meaning and value to be found in the Christian life. Christianity does not recognize different spheres of activity in the logotherapeutic sense, but rather, only different modes of activity within the one sphere.

These divergent viewpoints are not necessarily contradictory, however, for Logotherapy as a scientific psychotherapeutic system intends to proceed only to the "boundaries of transcendence" and, while not committed to any religious system specifically, to remain "open" to all systems, such as Christianity, which repudiate an exclusively psychodynamic view of man, and recognize the spiritual dimension of human existence. On the other hand, the Christian therapist has already committed himself on the other side of the "boundary" and, therefore, includes the revelational data in his psychotherapeutic perspective.

It is in this area of the therapeutic goals of the medical ministry of Logotherapy that there is, perhaps, the most difference between Logotherapy and the Christian faith. As has been pointed out, however, Frankl is consistent with his presuppositions derived from his existential analysis of human existence, while the biblical perspective, based upon the presumed revelation from God, makes a specific system of values a definite part of the "ministry" to the spiritual dimension of man.

The Christian therapist, whenever an objective realm of meaning and values enter the therapeutic relationship, has a direct responsibility to present, as a possible option, the meaning and value of the Christian life. He must not, of course, attempt to impose this upon the patient, nor attempt to "transfer" (or, perhaps better said, counter-transfer) his personal religious experiences, but rather, he should trust that the patient, becoming aware of the potentialities in Christ, will be persuaded by God to make that personal, responsible, existential decision, the leap of faith, which is unto eternal life.

Whereas Logotherapy seeks to "broaden the value horizons" of the patient, so does the Christian therapist seek to

broaden the horizon, specifically to include the message of
hope and joy that is in the Christian gospel.

Frankl details[10] the task of the therapist as assisting the
patient to be able to work, to be able to enjoy life, and to be
able to suffer. He mentions that to be able to believe is in no
sense a therapeutic task, though it is occasionally an "acci-
dent" of psychotherapy. In a real sense, however, all of these
accomplishments are accidents of therapy, for the therapist is
dependent upon the grace of God for any improved condition. Certainly he has no power in himself to heal the patient.
One wonders why suffering is so important as over against
faith, in logotherapeutic teachings, inasmuch as suffering can
really only be borne through faith. It obviously cannot be
construed as an end in itself.

The logotherapeutic view of the relationship between psychotherapy and the religious commitment of the patient is
clearly set forth in the following quotation, in which Frankl
answers a question put to him concerning the "place of
grace" in Logotherapy:

"It is my opinion that a doctor should not flirt with Grace,
but that he should focus his attention, when he is prescrib-
ing, to the prescription, and when he is performing an operation, on the operation. And the more he is concerned with
the prescription and the operation, the better he will serve
the purpose of a vessel for Grace. We have to take care, as
medical doctors, that the interior room of the natural realm
is brought in order, and just take care that the doors to the
supernatural realm are not being locked, and locked by ourselves, but left open so that the patient can pass through
them, out of the whole spontaneity which is presupposed,
especially in his religious life. If the doctor would try to

---

[10] Frankl, MS, 59 ff.

shoulder the responsibility of answering the question of an
ultimate meaning of suffering, for instance, he would meet
difficulties."[11]

The Christian therapist, however, while not personally
shouldering the responsibility of the meaning of suffering, believes that it has been clearly set forth in the vicarious suffering of Jesus Christ. This is the theme that is the need of
the heart of the suffering patient. How to meet this need is
not easy, but the therapist who has met it himself, will have
a personal resource by means of which the patient may
glimpse the possibilities of his own fulfillment in Christ.

A biblical vocation of psychotherapy can be fulfilled only
with the overall therapeutic goal for the patient as a "man of
God, thoroughly furnished unto good works." Of course,
there are many psychotherapists who are also Christians, and
who would disagree with this point of view, but they cannot
in the true sense of the word be called "Christian therapists."
They are rather of that number among the Christian community whose occupation is both accidental and irrelevant
to their professed personal faith.

It is the conviction of the author that such persons not only
fail to see the deep need of the man in distress, but also fail to
realize the potentially powerful answer to this need in Christ.
The love of God, which has been "shed abroad" in their
hearts through their commitment of faith, will have the
same sustaining effect in the lives of their patients. When the
patient is content with a mere physical or psychological well
being as a state of life, it is the obligation of the Christian
therapist to help him to this level, but it is also the therapist's
obligation not to do the patient the disservice of appearing

---

[11] Cited from a lecture by Frankl at the University of Melbourne,
Australia, in October 1957.

to agree that psychophysical health is the highest value in life.

It may be that some will feel that viewpoint would restrict the practice of the Christian therapist to those persons of his own faith as a matter of ethical obligation. However, this only involves that he must not disguise his perspective, but instead, be careful that the patient realizes initially that he is consulting with a "Christian therapist." This may, in practice, restrict his clientele to those of the Christian faith, though this has not been true in the psychological counseling practice of the author.

In this connection, one should avoid the caricature of the therapist with a religious orientation based upon the Scriptures, as one who merely passes out religious literature, sprinkles an intolerant directive counseling with biblical phraseology, or uses the interview time in prayer (all of which, with the exception of the intolerant directiveness, may under some circumstances have an appropriate place). By the same token, the Christian therapist must not validate such a caricature, by assuming that his religious knowledge and experience may be an acceptable substitute for a thorough professional training.

E. Logotherapy and Christianity

In this chapter in which Logotherapy is related to Christianity, it is well to reflect upon whether they are in any valid sense comparable. Logotherapy is presented as a scientific psychotherapeutic theory based upon both empirical and phenomenological data, as well as the results of psychotherapeutic practice. Christianity, on the other hand, is a religious philosophy of life. The dividing line between science and philosophy becomes decidedly tenuous, however, when it is clear that both include a judgmental commitment about the data of experience, which is in no wise a part of that data. It is, rather, an act of faith.

Thus, in this sense, Logotherapy includes statements about a transcendent reality, about objective responsibility (instead of "felt" responsibility), about objective meaning and values, and about the objectivity of the world. All of these, obviously, are matters of faith, judgments as to the best accounting for the phenomenal data of human experience. This is in no sense disparaging, but, on the contrary, rather a recognition that science, if it is to be of value, must go beyond the mere listing of pointer readings, or data counts, to a philosophical commitment as to the meaning of the data.

In the light of this, Logotherapy and Christianity have much in common. However, whereas Logotherapy in its philosophical observations only affirms the existence of transcendent reality, the Bible reveals it. The basis for the objective responsibility of man is beyond the scope of Logotherapy, "to this question Existential Analysis is at a loss for the answer, the question remains open."[12] Christianity, however, asserts that the basis of responsibility is to the God of the Scriptures, who made heaven and earth. Logotherapy must remain agnostic about the objective "meaning of meaning" and all transcendent reality, "not only is man not able to comprehend the absolute meaning, but rather, he is also unable to know the Absolute in any other respect."[13] Christianity, to the contrary, affirms the possibility of an intimate personal (though, of course, not exhaustive) knowl-

---

[12] Frankl, LE, 41.
[13] Frankl, HP, 55.

edge of God in Jesus Christ.[14] Thus Christianity, a revealed theological world view, necessarily goes beyond Logotherapy, in its conclusions concerning the data of psychiatry.

Logotherapy makes a commitment in regard to human beings. "In the moral sense there are no races, or perhaps one should say only two 'races' . . . decent, and indecent human beings."[15] "In man are the possibilities to be an angel or a devil."[16] The Bible also asserts that there are only two proper classifications of humanity, the redeemed and the lost, the children of darkness and the children of light, those who believe in the Way, the Truth, and the Life, and those who do not.

Logotherapy also commits itself to a realistic view of objective moral values, which are not mere appearances, but rather, reality. "Between the true and the false as well as between the good and the evil, there is neither 'dialectic' nor 'synthesis,' but rather only decision."[17] Christianity, going beyond Logotherapy, maintains that this is true, and that while all men by nature choose the false and the evil, the true and the good are available through the commitment of faith to the person of Christ.

The Bible, just as it does with all areas of life, concerns itself with sickness. Sin is viewed as the background and ground for all human problems. There is no necessary connection between a man's illness and personal sinfulness, though a causal relation is frequently the case. The grace of

---

[14] Frankl does, however, speak of the mysterious simultaneity of absolute distance between God and man on the one hand; and, on the other hand, God's absolute intimate closeness and potential presence. Cf. Frankl, HP, 107 ff.

[15] Frankl, LE, 9-10.

[16] Frankl, LE,

[17] Frankl, MS, 85. Cited from Romano Guardini in *Religion, Wissenschaft, Kultur.*

God may be instrumental in healing the individual, whether the disease be primarily physical, psychological, or spiritual, or it may not. The decision is not determined by the degree of faith, but by the will of God. However, when healing does take place, the grace of God is at work, sometimes in mysterious "wonder" power, and sometimes through the seemingly mundane means of medication.

The Christian therapist, therefore, believes that all healing is, in the last analysis, an act of grace, and that every valid technique of therapy which may be found at his disposal is a means of grace, to be prayerfully and carefully used in the psychotherapeutic encounter. This does not necessarily entail "spiritualism," for the source of the illness may be in any dimension of the personality, and should be regarded and treated as such. However, it does entail the belief, common with Logotherapy, that man is a unity, and that the dimensions are really not separate compartments, but rather, aspects of an interrelated complex unity which may be observed through the various facets of physique, psyche, and spirit, for the purpose of analysis. The true meaning of life, therefore, the message of Christ, will have a most salutary effect in "de-reflecting" the individual to objective meaning and values. It may also, through the reconciliation of the spirit of man to God, bring about a harmony that will, as a side effect, adjust defects in the psychophysicum. Thus, though the Christian faith is not to be considered as a mere psychotherapeutic tool, it has, nonetheless, remarkable psychotherapeutic value.

In Logotherapy, the spiritual dimension of man is held to be inviolable, impervious to defect or disease. In the Bible it is viewed, in its natural state, as being plagued with a serious sickness, the state of sin. This does not necessarily prevent his making existential decisions in reference to his psychophysicum, but it does prohibit his fulfilling his responsibility. It leads him to guilt and despair, and often permeates his whole personality with existential frustration or existential vacuum.

The rectification of this state is not within the possibility of the Christian therapist, just as the possibility of healing any defective state is inherently beyond his competence. However, he still is ready to serve as the means of grace for the solution of this, the great problem of life, as well as for the solution of neurotic, and other pressing problems of the personal and social existence of the individual.

In the area of unavoidable suffering, the Bible offers the comfort and solace of eternity with God as the objective ground for which Logotherapy, at best, can offer only a vague existential hope. Man can endure every hardship, and every tribulation that his destiny dictates when he can, by faith, affirm with the Apostle Paul that the "suffering of this present time cannot be compared with the glory that will be revealed." It is a most significant contribution of Logotherapy to emphasize the value potentiality of necessary suffering, but it is only the biblical world view which gives it its rationale.

The Christian psychotherapist has a comprehensive commitment far beyond the restricted realm of psychotherapy. It is no mean task and one to be carefully considered before one "puts his hands to the plow." He will find, I believe, that he will have invaluable aids along the way, not the least of which is Logotherapy.

Logotherapy, as a psychotherapeutic theory and therapy, is making effective headway in a new direction which restores humanity to the patient, and calls upon his powerful existential potentialities in the alleviation of his neurotic problems.

The Christian therapist will be wise to utilize its valuable contributions to his therapeutic vocation. Although the analogy is imperfect, the relationship of Logotherapy to the Christian psychotherapeutic vocation, is similar to that of the Old Testament to the complete biblical revelation.[18] It points in the true direction, but does not arrive at the true destination.

In conclusion, the brief analysis of Logotherapy in this volume has revealed a concept of man, of human motivation, and a psychotherapeutic approach, which are in refreshing contrast to the theories and practices based upon a materialistic, mechanistic presupposition which pervades a large area of the field of mental health. Logotherapy, while not being a religious system, gives an honest appraisal of the religious factors of human existence, as well as the spiritual dimension of man from which they stem. When related to the specific religious system of a Christian *Weltanschauung* based upon the biblical data, it, as a phenomenological analysis of human existence and an empirically validated psychotherapeutic theory, is seen to be of inestimable value in its complementation. However, the therapist whose presuppositions are grounded in the biblical revelation, in which is presented a specific view of God and His purpose for each individual man, must, in reference to this revelation, go beyond the logotherapeutic teachings in order to satisfy the responsibility entailed in a biblical vocation. He will be greatly encouraged by Frankl's work and will, perhaps, consider it an honor to be numbered with the logotherapists, while at the same time being under no illusion that the converse will be true.

---

[18] Cf. Köberle, "Psychotherapie und Seelsorge," in *Die Psychotherapie in der Gegenwart* (ed. by E. Stern), Rascher Verlag, Zürich, 1958, p. 374.

BIBLIOGRAPHY

Bibliography of Frankl's Works Frequently Cited in this Volume

(AS) — *Ärztliche Seelsorge*, Verlag Franz Deuticke, Wien, 1952.

(DS) — *The Doctor and the Soul*, Alfred A. Knopf, New York, 1957.

(HB) — *Handbuch der Neurosenlehre und Psychotherapie*, Urban & Schwarzenberg, Wien, 1957.

(HP) — *Homo Patiens*, Verlag Franz Deuticke, Wien, 1950.

(LE) — *Logos und Existenz*, Amandus-Verlag, Wien, 1951.

(MS) — *Das Menschenbild der Seelenheilkunde*, Hippokrates-Verlag, Stuttgart, 1959.

(PP) — *Die Psychotherapie in der Praxis*, Verlag Franz Deuticke, Wien, 1947.

(TT) — *Theorie und Therapie der Neurosen*, Urban & Schwarzenberg, Wien, 1956.

(UG) — *Der Unbewusste Gott*, Amandus-Verlag, Wien, 1949.

(UM) — *Der Unbedingte Mensch*, Verlag Franz Deuticke, Wien, 1949.

(ZV) — *Zeit und Verantwortung*, Verlag Franz Deuticke, Wien, 1947.

Bibliography of Logotherapeutic Literature in English

Ansbacher, Rowena R.: "The Third Viennese School of Psychotherapy," *Journal of Individual Psychology*, 15: 236-237 (1959).

Arnold, Magda B., and John A. Gasson: *The Human Person,* New York: Ronald Press, 1954, Chapter 16: "Logotherapy and Existential Analysis."

Frankl, Viktor E.: *The Doctor and the Soul,* An Introduction to Logotherapy, New York: Alfred A. Kopf, 1955-1957.

Frankl, Viktor E.: *From Death-Camp to Existentialism,* A Psychiatrist's Path to a New Therapy, Preface by Gordon A. Allport, Boston: Beacon Press, 1959.

Frankl, Viktor E.: *Existence and Values,* Foundations of Logotherapy and Existential Analysis, New York: Harper Brothers (in preparation).

Frankl, Viktor E.: "Logotherapy and the Collective Neuroses," in: *Progress in Psychotherapy,* Vol IV, edited by J. H. Masserman and J. L. Moreno, New York: Grune & Stratton, 1959.

Frankl, Viktor E.: In *Critical Incidents in Psychotherapy,* edited by S. W. Standal and R. J. Corsini, Englewood Cliffs: Prentice-Hall, 1959.

Frankl, Viktor E.: "On Logotherapy and Existential Analysis," *American Journal of Psychoanalysis,* 18: 28-37 (1958). (Paper read before the Association for the Advancement of Psychoanalysis in New York on April 17, 1957).

Frankl, Viktor E.: "The Spiritual Dimension in Existential Analysis and Logotherapy," *Journal of Individual Psychology,* 15: 157-165 (1959). (Paper read before the Fourth International Congress of Psychotherapy in Barcelona, Spain, on September 5, 1958).

Frankl, Viktor E.: "From Psychotherapy to Logotherapy," *Pastoral Psychology,* 7: 56-60 (1956).

Frankl, Viktor E.: "Logos and Existence in Psychotherapy," *American Journal of Psychotherapy,* 7: 8-15 (1953).

Frankl, Viktor E.: "The Will to Meaning," *The Journal of Pastoral Care,* 12: 82-88 (1958).

Frankl, Viktor E.: "The Concept of Man in Psychotherapy," *Pastoral Psychology,* 6: 16-26 (1955). (Paper read before the Royal Society of Medicine, Section of Psychiatry, in London, England, on June 15, 1954).

Frankl, Viktor E.: "Group Therapeutic Experiences in a Concentration Camp," *Group Psychotherapy*, 7: 81-90 (1954). (Paper read before the Second International Congress of Psychotherapy in Leiden, Netherlands, on September 8, 1951).

Frankl, Viktor E.: "Guest Editorial," *Academy Reporter* (Academy of Religion and Mental Health), Vol. 3, No. 5, May 1958.

Frankl, Viktor E.: "Religion and Existential Psychotherapy," *The Gordon Review*, Vol. 6, Spring-Summer, 1960.

Frankl, Viktor E.: "Beyond Self-Actualization and Self-Expression," *Journal of Existential Psychiatry*, Vol. 1, No. 1, Spring, 1960.

Frankl, Viktor E.: "Paradoxical Intention, A Logotherapeutic Technique," *American Journal of Psychotherapy*, Vol. XIV, No. 3, July 1960.

Frankl, Viktor E.: "Logotherapy and the Challenge of Suffering," *Review of Existential Psychology and Psychiatry*, Vol. I, No. 1, 1960.

Polak, Paul: "Frankl's Existential Analysis," *American Journal of Psychotherapy*, 3: 617-622 (1949).

VanderVeldt, James H., and Robert P. Odenwald: *Psychiatry and Catholicism*, New York: McGraw-Hill, 1952, Chapter 8, "Existential Analysis."

Weisskopf-Joelson, Edith: "Logotherapy and Existential Analysis," *Acts Psychotherapeutica*, 6: 193-204 (1958).

Weisskopf-Joelson, Edith: "Some Comments on a Viennese School of Psychiatry," *Journal of Abnormal and Social Psychology*, 51: 701-703 (1955).

Author Index